TaeKwonDo - The Art of 태권도

Volume 1
The Illustrated Guide to TAEGEUK Forms

By Jessica Mandel and Alex Man

Illustrated by Alex Man

II

Table of Contents

Introduction — 1
- Taekwondo – a general look — 1

First Part - Forms / Poomsae — 2

Theory — 2
- Basic principals in doing the forms — 2
- Advantages of learning and practicing the forms — 2
- Learning process — 3
- Breathing during forms — 3
- The Taegeuk forms — 3
- The Trigrams — 4
- Additional Information — 5

Illustrations of the forms

Taegeuk form 1 - (Taegeuk Il Jang) — 7
- A one-page glance at the entire sequence of movements — 9
- The form in the context of the entire pattern — 10
- The form with English names of each technique — 11
- Detailed information, including multiple views and naming in both English and Korean (phonetically) — 13

Taegeuk form 2 - (Taegeuk Yi Jang) — 19
- A one-page glance at the entire sequence of movements — 21
- The form in the context of the entire pattern — 22
- The form with English names of each technique — 23
- Detailed information, including multiple views and naming in both English and Korean (phonetically) — 25

Taegeuk form 3 - (Taegeuk Sam Jang) — 33
- A one-page glance at the entire sequence of movements — 35
- The form in the context of the entire pattern — 36
- The form with English names of each technique — 37
- Detailed information, including multiple views and naming in both English and Korean (phonetically) — 39

Taegeuk form 4 - (Taegeuk Sa Jang)   49
- A one-page glance at the entire sequence of movements   51
- The form in the context of the entire pattern   52
- The form with English names of each technique   53
- Detailed information, including multiple views and naming in both English and Korean (phonetically)   55

Taegeuk form 5 - (Taegeuk Oh Jang)   63
- A one-page glance at the entire sequence of movements   65
- The form in the context of the entire pattern   66
- The form with English names of each technique   67
- Detailed information, including multiple views and naming in both English and Korean (phonetically)   69

Taegeuk form 6 - (Taegeuk Yuk Jang)   79
- A one-page glance at the entire sequence of movements   81
- The form in the context of the entire pattern   82
- The form with English names of each technique   83
- Detailed information, including multiple views and naming in both English and Korean (phonetically)   85

Taegeuk form 7 - (Taegeuk Chil Jang)   95
- A one-page glance at the entire sequence of movements   97
- The form in the context of the entire pattern   98
- The form with English names of each technique   99
- Detailed information, including multiple views and naming in both English and Korean (phonetically)   101

Taegeuk form 8 - (Taegeuk Pal Jang)   111
- A one-page glance at the entire sequence of movements   113
- The form in the context of the entire pattern   114
- The form with English names of each technique   115
- Detailed information, including multiple views and naming in both English and Korean (phonetically)   118

Second Part – Techniques and More — 129

Basic and advanced techniques — 129
- Basic and advanced stances — 130
- Basic and advanced blocks — 132
- Strikes and punches — 135
- Basic and advanced kicks — 137

Animals in Taekwondo — 139
- Stances — 140
- Hand techniques and kicks — 141

About the authors — 143

Introduction

A general look at Taekwondo and the forms:

Taekwondo is a Korean traditional martial art which is now an Olympic sport. Taekwondo includes blocks, punches, hand attacks, kicks, and much more.

Taekwondo is composed of 5 basic elements:
- Self-defense (hoshinsul)
- Athletic fights (kyrougi)
- Breaking (kyopka)
- Working on basic techniques
- Forms (poomsae)

Forms / Poomsae are composed of blocks and attacks which the students practice. A form is a sequence of pre-arranged fight moves against a number of imaginary opponents.
By practicing forms, the Taekwondo practitioner develops:
- Speed
- Flow of movements
- Timing
- Power
- Good technical understanding of the techniques
- How to breathe correctly in Taekwondo
- Concentration

During advanced stages, it may be used as a sort of meditation via movement.

In the preliminary stages, one learns the movements and the directions in the form (poomsae) and knows the whole pattern by heart.

The second stage is done by going over the characteristics of each technique and over the flow of the movements in the form.

First Part - Forms / Poomsae:

Theory:

Basic principals in doing the Taegeuk forms:
1. While you are performing the forms, you must keep focused and do each technique with power and determination.
2. Each technique is to be done precisely and well.
3. All the forms start and finish at precisely the same spot.
4. You are to know each technique that is to be done and know its application. Additionally, you must know where each technique is aimed regarding height, direction, angle and know which part of the body is used in order to perform the attack or block.
5. You must always turn your head and look before you do a technique. As the form is an imaginary fight against a number of opponents, it is, therefore, logical to look before you do a technique of blocking or attacking.
6. Each technique (block, punch, strike, or kick) must be done with determination, precision, and power, yet the form as a whole must be done flowingly, a balance of power and calm. Therefore one must relax the body between movements.
7. You must keep your stability, especially with kicks and turns, otherwise the body tends to lose balance.
8. Kihap (yelling) – make sure you do the Kihap paired with the correct technique. The Kihap will take place while performing the technique and not prior to or after performing it.
9. Rhythm – forms have a basic rhythm which should not be too fast and allows you to do each technique with power and precision whilst paying attention to balance and correct breathing. In addition to the basic rhythm, there are parts which are done slower – again, paying strict attention to the breath, and some parts that are done faster – which are usually a combination of a number of techniques of blocking and attacking, for the emphasis on power and strength.

Advantages of learning and practicing the forms:
- It can be done anywhere. you do not need anything besides a flat area and some space.
- You can do it on your own – you do not need a partner.
- You do not need any special equipment.
- It is suitable for kids, adults, the elderly or when you are injured and should avoid Taekwondo fighting.
- It is suitable for those who are not interested in fighting.

The Process of Learning Forms:
The studying and learning of forms happen in a few stages.
The first stage is to learn the structure of the form – the pattern. The second stage, after you know the entire structure, start to work and fix each and every technique. The third stage (which may take place even before learning the form itself) is when you practice each individual technique over and over again until you do it the best you can. Of course, you must be sure that you understand and know the application of each technique. The final stage is when you review and practice the form over and over again while paying attention to the quality of each technique, the timing of breathing, the rhythm, the power and so on. This stage takes years!

Remember, practicing forms is a long process, built up on repetition and ongoing training that never ends. There is always room for improvement.

Breathing During Forms:
Breathing is a very important in general and during form practice in particular.
Correct breathing allows you to maintain your energy for the duration of a fight, form practice, and adds power to each technique you do.
The majority of each form is performed at a steady pace, with the exception of a few slow and fast parts. We inhale in preparation for a technique and exhale as we execute it, be it a punch, hand attack, kick or block. We inhale through the nose and exhale through the mouth.

The Taegeuk Forms:
There are 8 forms which you learn before the black belt.
You start with the first form (Taegeuk Il Jang). And as you advance, the
second and thus onwards according to your advancing level and student rank. Up
to the 8th form (Taegeuk Pal Jang) which you learn before the promotion test to
black belt. "Taegeuk" is the Korean name of the Yin Yang sign – "the supreme ultimate".

The Yin Yang is a definition which belongs to the ancient Asian philosophy,
Two opposing but complementary forces that can be found in all things in the universe.
Yin – is the cold, shaded, materialistic and receiving part.
Yang – is the warm, lit, energetic and giving part.
Yin Yang can be represented in many different ways, another way is:
A straight line represents Yang
A broken line represents Yin

The Trigrams:

A combination of 3 Yin Yangs together is called a trigram.
There are 8 trigrams.
Each trigram shows a process or an element in nature.
Each Taegeuk form represents 1 of the 8 trigrams.

Form number	Nature	Trigram name	Trigram	Represents
Taegeuk number 1 (Taegeuk Il Jang)	Heaven and Light	Keon	☰	Creation
Taegeuk number 2 (Taegeuk Yi Jang)	Lake	Tae	☱	Joyfulness
Taegeuk number 3 (Taegeuk Sam Jang)	Fire and Sun	Ri	☲	Warmth, enthusiasm, hope
Taegeuk number 4 (Taegeuk Sa Jang)	Thunder and Lightning	Jin	☳	Bravery
Taegeuk number 5 (Taegeuk Oh Jang)	Wind	Seon	☴	Humble state of mind
Taegeuk number 6 (Taegeuk Yuk Jang)	Water	Gam	☵	Confidence
Taegeuk number 7 (Taegeuk Chil Jang)	Mountain	Gan	☶	"Top Stop" know when to stop
Taegeuk number 8 (Taegeuk Pal Jang)	Earth	Gon	☷	Receptive

Additional Information:

Each and every form starts with a ready stance (chonbi) and finishes with a ready stance precisely at the same place where you started.
In many Taekwondo clubs there are a few steps prior to starting practicing:
• Standing in an attention stance (charyot).
• Bowing (kyongre).
• Declaring the name of the form, then moving to the ready stance (chonbi) and starting the form.
• At the end of the form, moving to attention stance (charyot) and bowing again.

In this book, we give the general principles which will apply to all Taekwondo students. With this in mind, each Taekwondo club has its own rules and regulations and pays closer attention to different principles. Thus there will be differences in approach between different clubs.
Also, there may be disparities between our book to what is taught in your club.
Our book comes to assist and give a comprehensive review of the forms but in no way is to replace the knowledge which is provided to you by your instructor.
Respect your instructor, be attentive, and absorb as much knowledge as possible.

Terms and meanings in Korean:
In different sources, we can find the Taekwondo terminology spelled in different variations since it's translated from Korean.
For example the term "ready stance" appears in a lot of variations:
Joon Bi
Junbi
Chonbi
Chunbi
Chunbi sogi / seogi / sugi
Thus, in the book, we tried to always make the correct choice to the best of
our knowledge and understanding when we wrote the techniques' name in Korean.

In some Taekwondo clubs, the back hand punch and the front hand punch terms are opposite. Sometimes they are called "bandai jireugi" and sometimes they are called "baro jireugi". In this book, we call the back hand punch a reverse punch (baro jireugi), and the front hand punch a punch (bandai jireugi).

Taegeuk Form 1 (Taegeuk Il Jang)

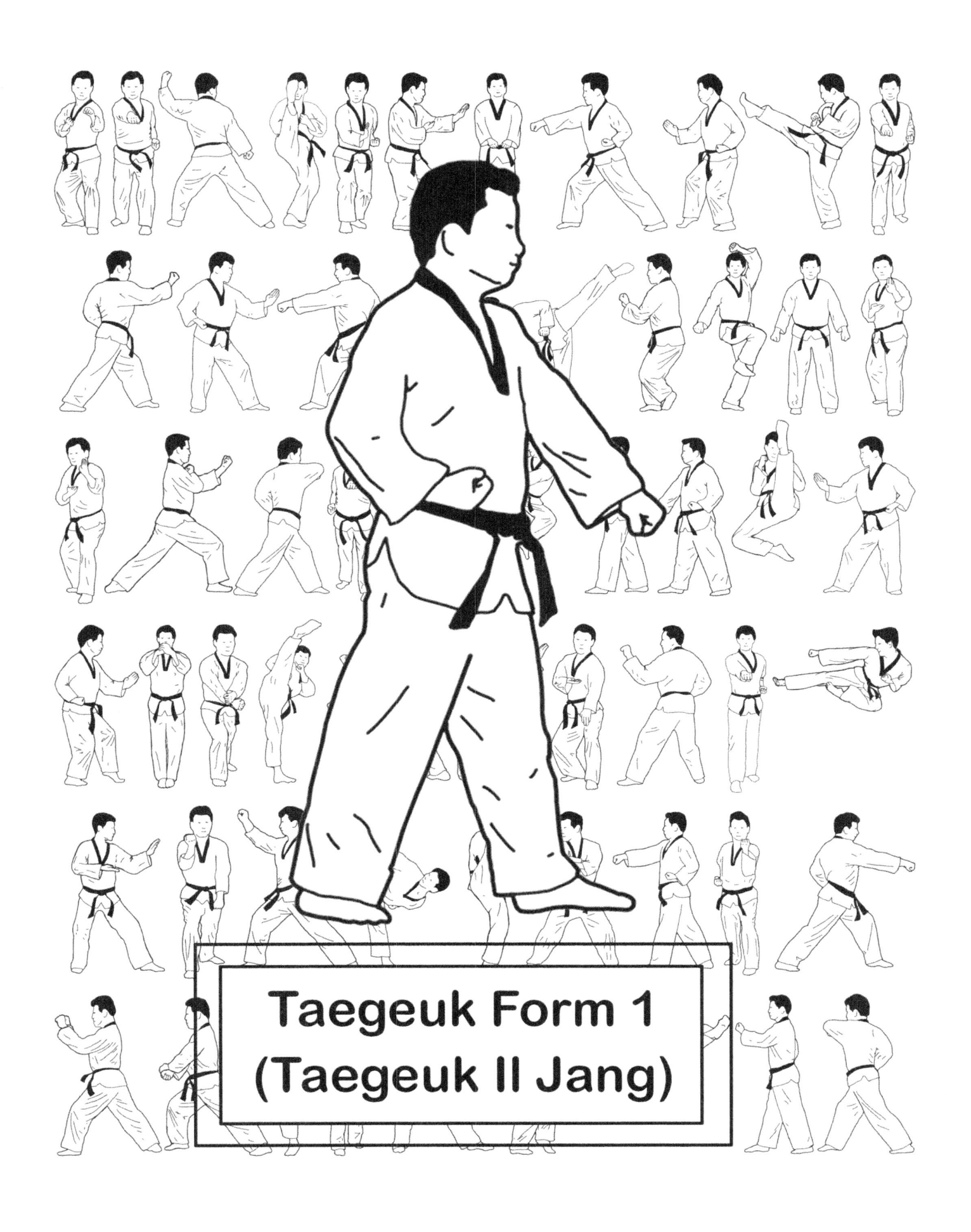

TAEGEUK IL JANG (1)

TAEGEUK IL JANG (1)

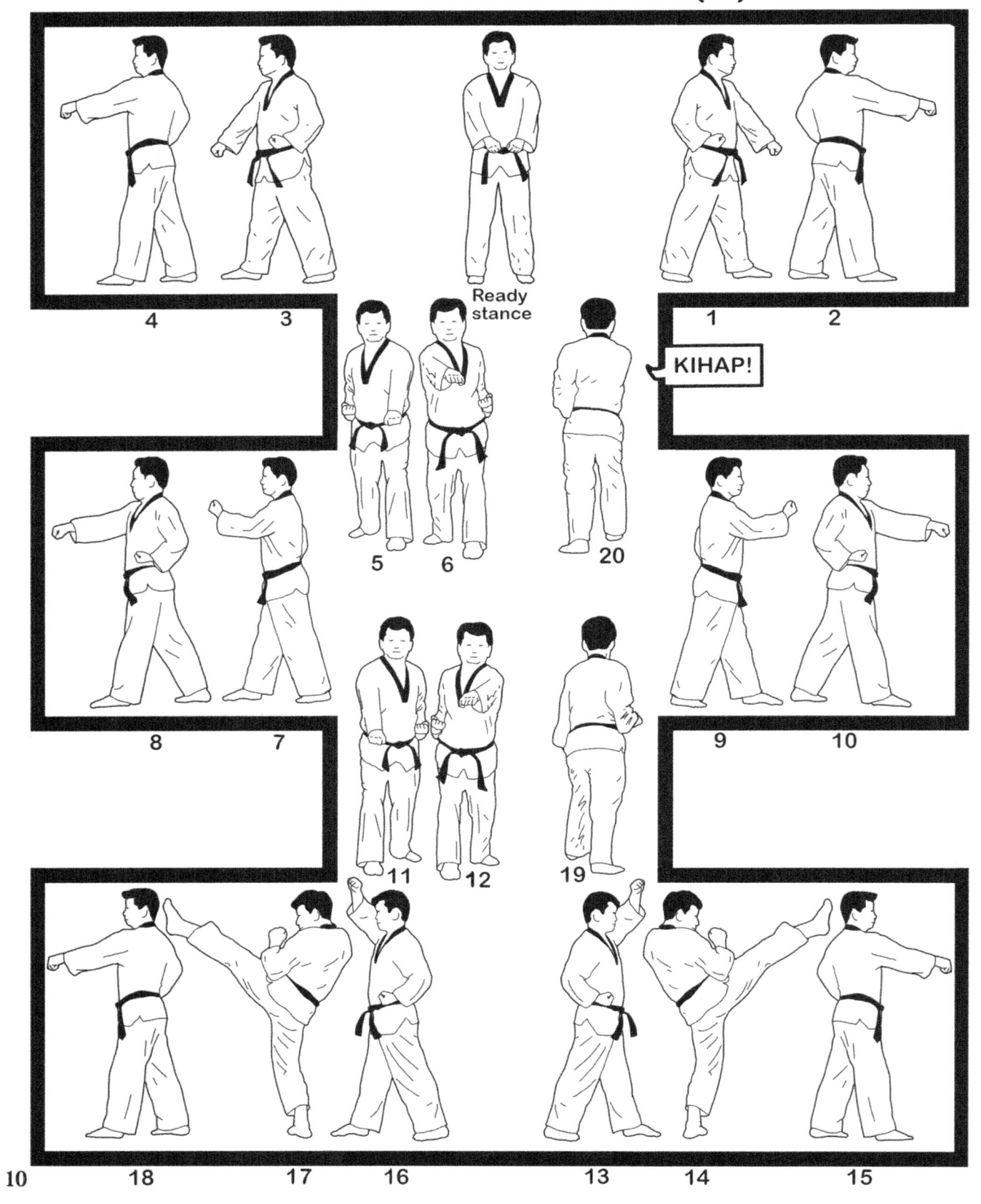

TAEGEUK IL JANG (1) PART ONE

Ready stance

1. Walking stance, low block
2. Walking stance, middle punch 
3. Walking stance, low block 
4. Walking stance, middle punch 
5A. Front stance, low block 
5B. Front stance, reverse middle punch 
6. Walking stance, reverse middle block 
7. Walking stance, reverse middle punch 
8. Walking stance, reverse middle block 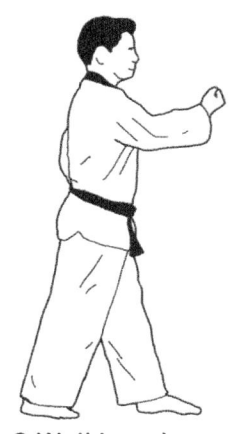
9. Walking stance, reverse middle punch 
10A. Front stance, low block 
10B. Front stance, reverse middle punch 
11. Walking stance, high block 
12. Front kick

TAEGEUK IL JANG (1) PART TWO

13. Walking stance, middle punch

14. Walking stance, high block

15. Front kick

16. Walking stance, middle punch

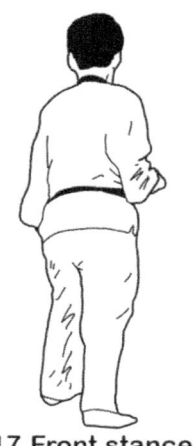

17. Front stance, low block  — Back view

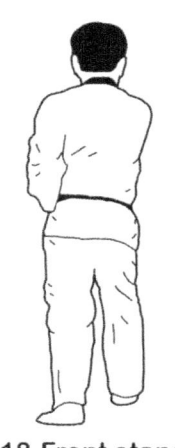

18. Front stance, middle punch  — Back view

KIHAP!

Ready stance

B ———— A
C ———— D
F ———— E

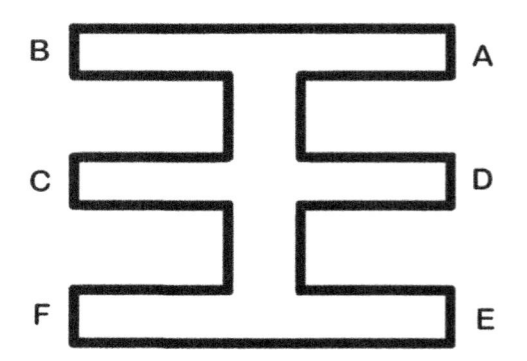

TAEGEUK IL JANG (1)

Philosophical symbol is -Keon- signifying light and heaven.

This poomsae is basic and suitable for yellow belts, geup 8-9 and up.

Basic blocks: low block, center block, high block.

Basic attacks – front kick and a punch to the center.

1. Ready stance (chonbi) legs parallel, hip width (naranhi sugi).

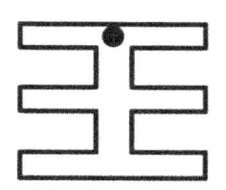

2.  To your left - walking stance (apsugi), low block (arehmakki). Keep the block about a fist above the leg.

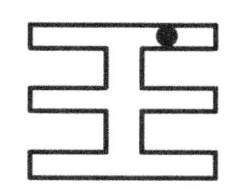

3.  Walking stance (apsugi) middle punch (momtong bandai jireugi). Keep the punch aimed at the solar plexus.

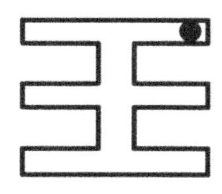

TAEGEUK IL JANG (1)

4. To your right - walking stance (apsugi),

low block (arehmakki).

Keep the block about a fist above the leg.

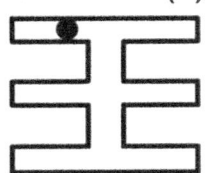

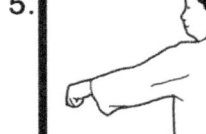

5.  Walking stance (apsugi),

middle punch

(momtong bandai jireugi).

Keep the punch aimed at the solar plexus.

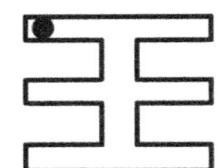

6.  Forward -

front stance (apkubi),

low block (arehmakki).

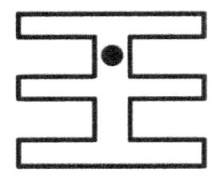

7.  Same stance –

front stance (apkubi),

reverse middle punch

(momtong baro jireugi).

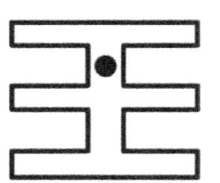

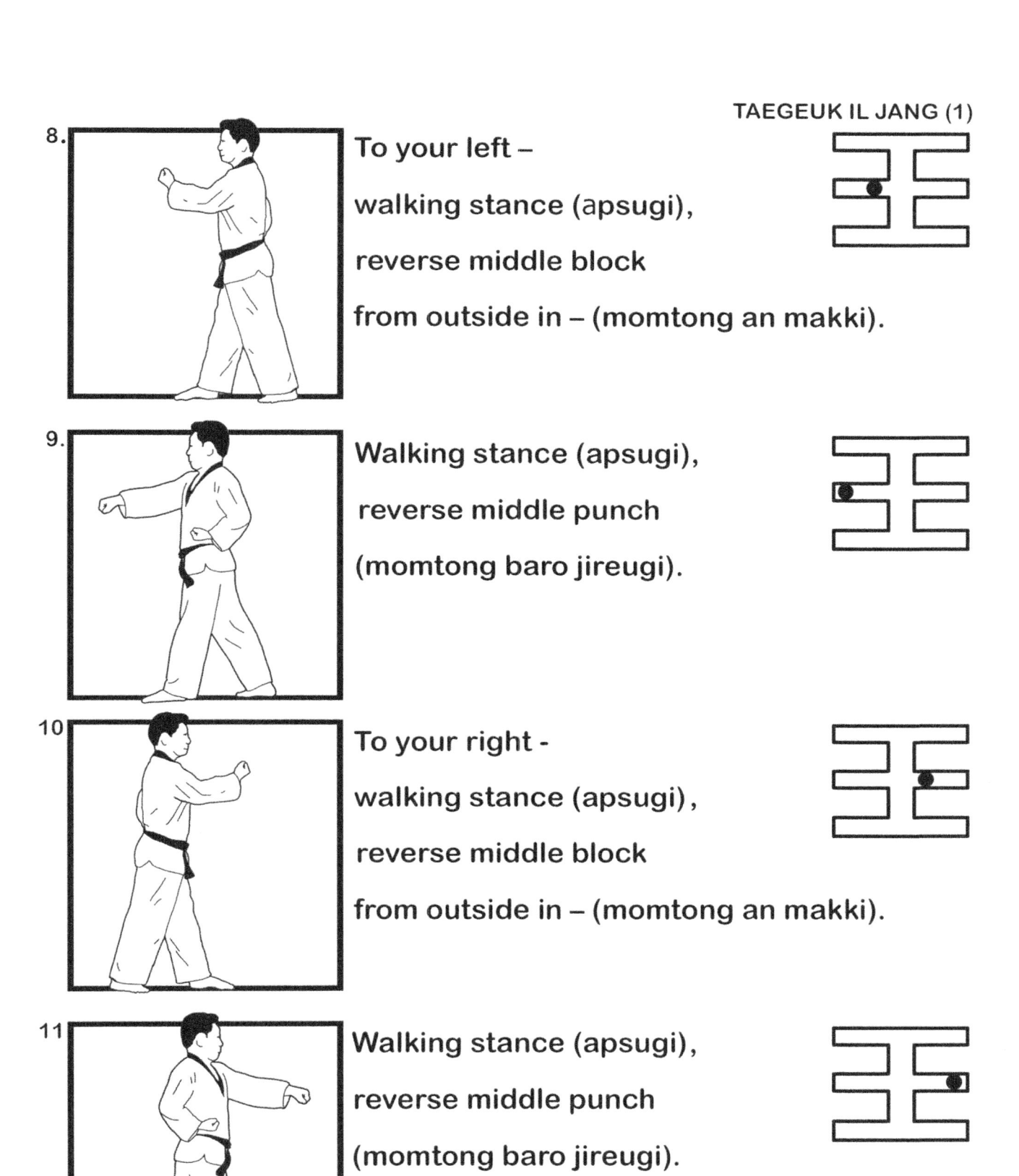

TAEGEUK IL JANG (1)

8. To your left –

walking stance (apsugi),

reverse middle block

from outside in – (momtong an makki).

9. Walking stance (apsugi),

reverse middle punch

(momtong baro jireugi).

10. To your right -

walking stance (apsugi),

reverse middle block

from outside in – (momtong an makki).

11. Walking stance (apsugi),

reverse middle punch

(momtong baro jireugi).

15

TAEGEUK IL JANG (1)

12. Forward –

front stance (apkubi),

low block (arehmakki).

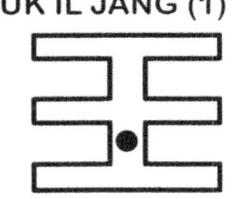

13.  Same stance –

front stance (apkubi),

reverse middle punch

(momtong baro jireugi).

14.  To your left –

walking stance (apsugi),

high block (ulgul makki).

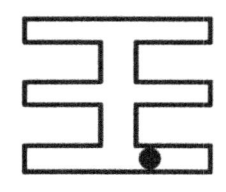

15.  Front kick (apchuck ap chagi).

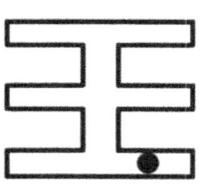

TAEGEUK IL JANG (1)

16. Landing in walking stance (apsugi), middle punch (momtong bandai jireugi).

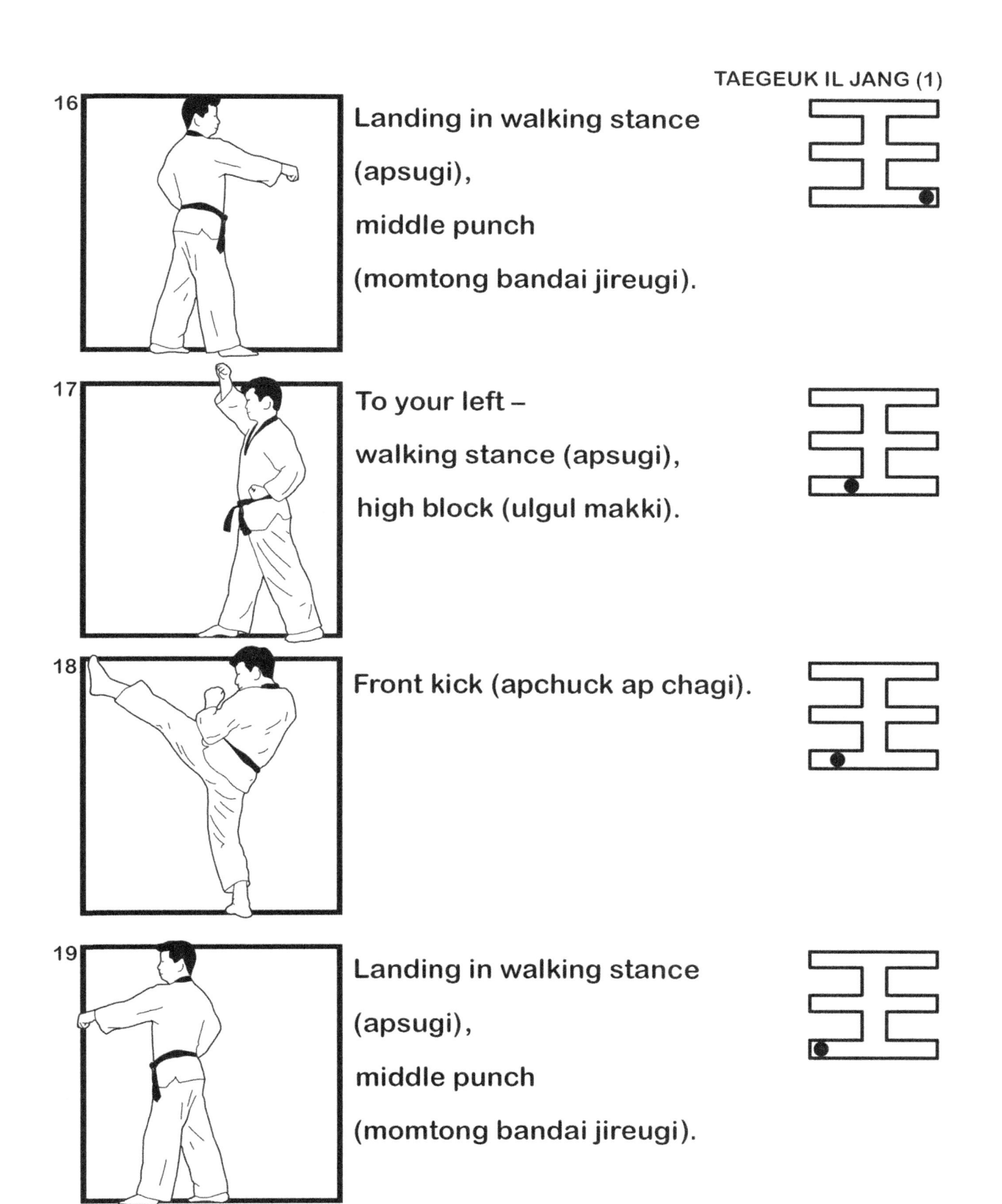

17. To your left – walking stance (apsugi), high block (ulgul makki).

18. Front kick (apchuck ap chagi).

19. Landing in walking stance (apsugi), middle punch (momtong bandai jireugi).

TAEGEUK IL JANG (1)

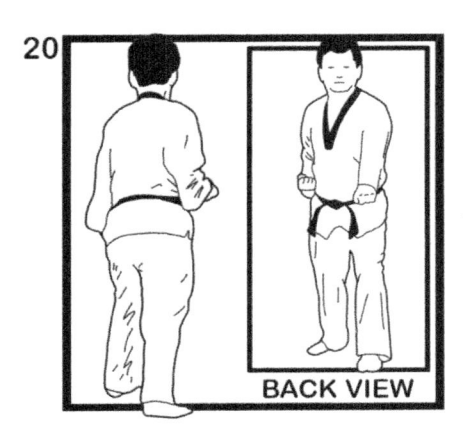

20 Backwards - (towards starting position) front stance (apkubi), low block (areh makki).

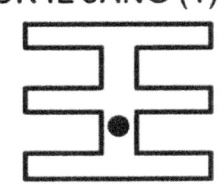

21 KIHAP! Backwards - (towards starting position) front stance (apkubi), middle punch (momtong bandai jireugi). Yell!

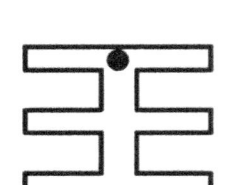

22 Turn your left foot to ready stance (chonbi) legs parallel, hip width (naranhi sugi).

Taegeuk Form 2 (Taegeuk Yi Jang)

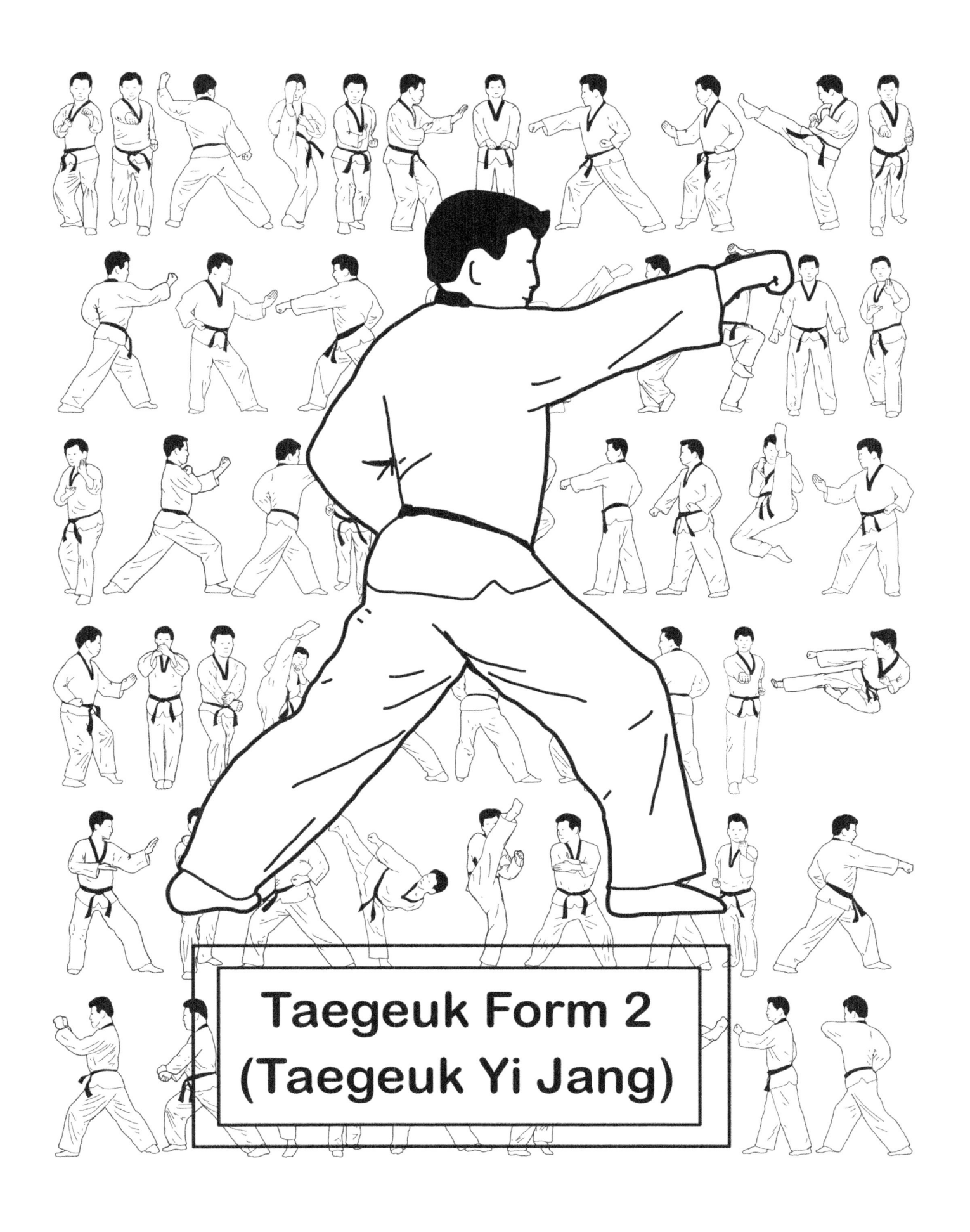

TAEGEUK YI JANG (2)

Ready stance | 1 | 2 | 3 | 4 | 5 | 6
7 | 8 | 9 | 10 | 11 | 12 | 13
14 | 15 | 16 | 17 | 18 | 19 | 20
21 | 22 | 23 (KIHAP!) | Ready stance

```
B ▬▬▬▬▬▬▬▬▬ A
D ▬▬▬▬▬▬▬▬▬ C
E ▬▬▬▬▬▬▬▬▬ F
```

21

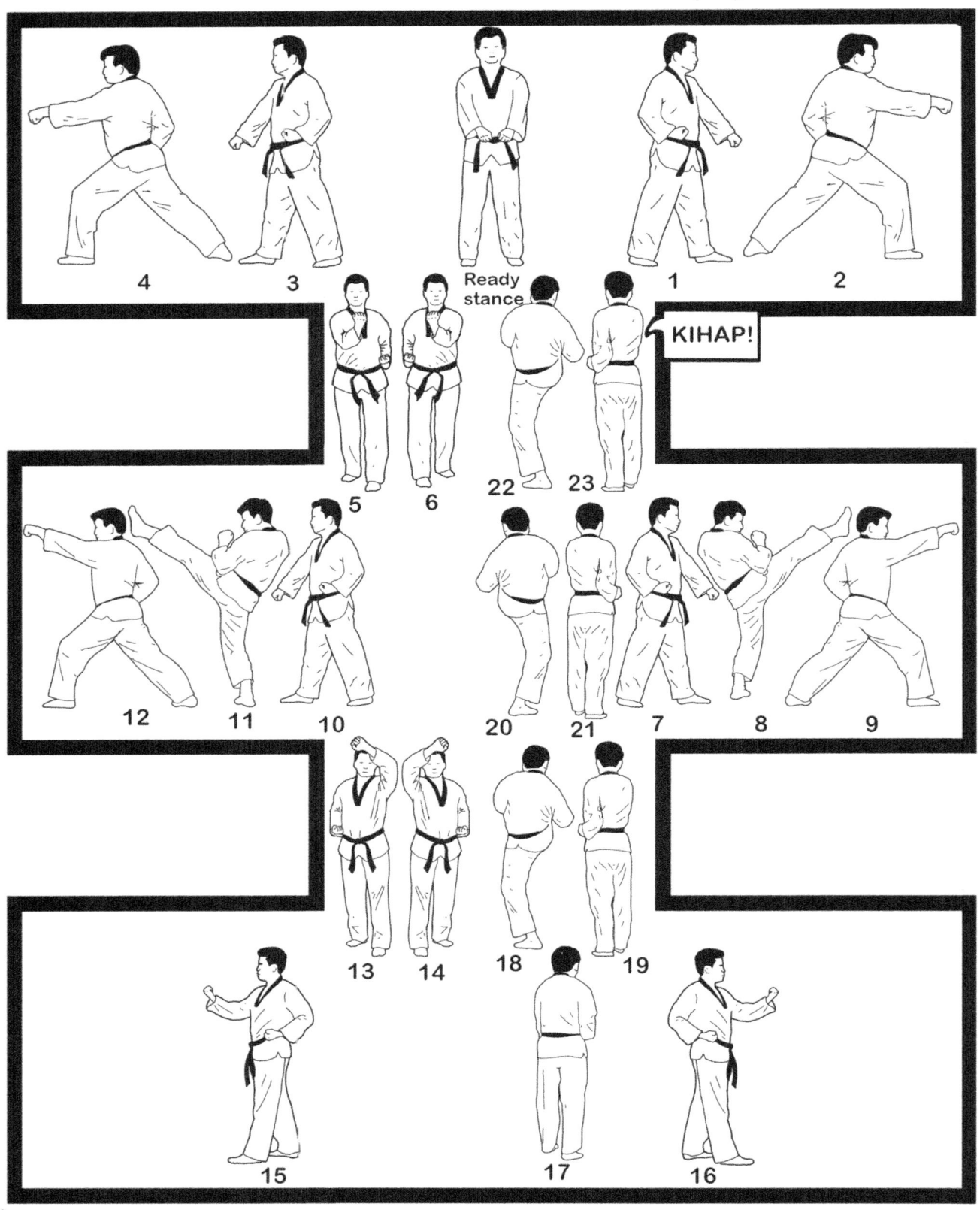

TAEGEUK YI JANG (2)

TAEGEUK YI JANG (2) PART ONE

1. Ready stance
2. Walking stance, low block
3. Front stance, middle punch
4. Walking stance, low block
5. Front stance, middle punch
6. Walking stance, reverse middle block
7. Walking stance, reverse middle block
8. Walking stance, low block
9. Front kick
10. Front stance, high punch
11. Walking stance, low block
12. Front kick
13. Front stance, high punch
14. Walking stance, high block
15. Walking stance, high block

TAEGEUK YI JANG (2) PART TWO

16. Walking stance, reverse middle block

17. Walking stance, reverse middle block

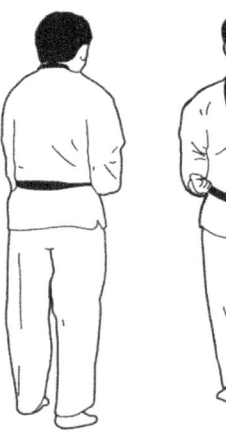

18. Walking stance, low block (Back view)

19. Front kick (Back view)

20. Walking (Back view) stance, middle punch

21. Front kick (Back view)

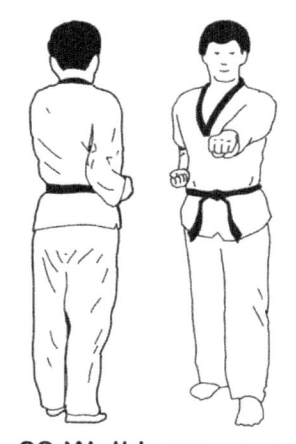

22. Walking (Back view) stance, middle punch

23. Front kick (Back view)

24. Walking (Back view) stance, middle punch

KIHAP!

25. Ready stance

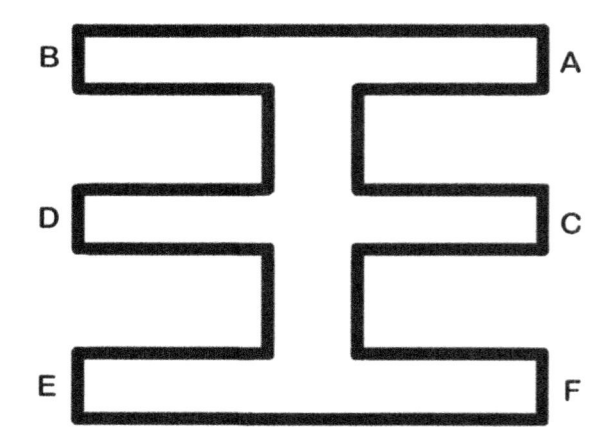

TAEGEUK YI JANG (2)

Philosophical symbol is - Tae - meaning joyfulness.

Regarding nature – a lake.

This poomsae is basic and is suitable for orange belts, geup 7 and up.

Basic stances – walking stance and front stance.

Basic blocks – low, center and high block.

Basic attacks – central punch and high punch.

1. Ready stance (chonbi) legs parallel, hip width (naranhi sugi).

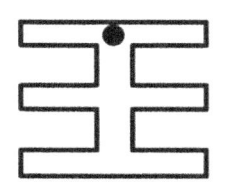

2.  To your left - walking stance (apsugi), low block (arehmakki). Keep the block about a fist above the leg.

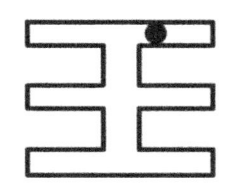

3.  Front stance (apkubi), middle punch (momtong bandai jireugi). Keep the punch aimed at the solar plexus.

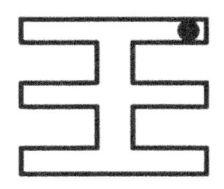

TAEGEUK YI JANG (2)

4.  To your right - walking stance (apsugi), low block (arehmakki). Keep the block about a fist above the leg.

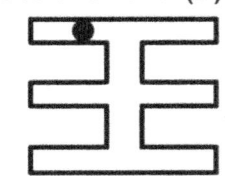

5.  Front stance (apkubi), middle punch (momtong bandai jireugi). Keep the punch aimed at the solar plexus.

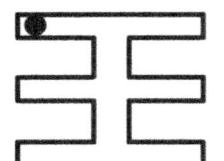

6.  Forward - walking stance (apsugi), reverse middle block (momtong an makki).

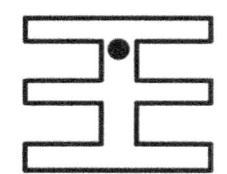

7.  Forward - walking stance (apsugi), reverse middle block (momtong an makki).

26

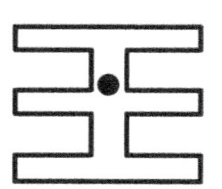

TAEGEUK YI JANG (2)

8. To your left - walking stance (apsugi), low block (arehmakki). Keep the block about a fist above the leg.

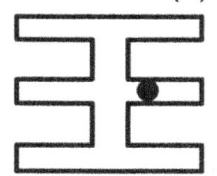

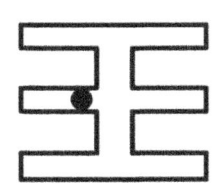

9. Front kick (apchuck ap chagi).

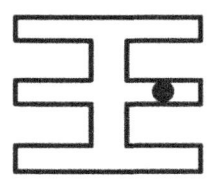

10. Front stance (apkubi), high punch (ulgul bandai jireugi).

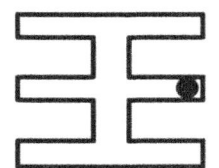

11. To your right - walking stance (apsugi), low block (arehmakki). Keep the block about a fist above the leg.

TAEGEUK YI JANG (2)

12. Front kick (apchuck ap chagi).

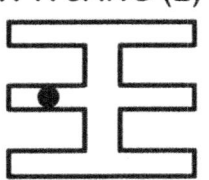

13.  Front stance (apkubi),

    high punch (ulgul bandai jireugi).

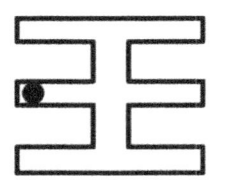

14.  Forward -

    walking stance (apsugi),

    high block (ulgul makki).

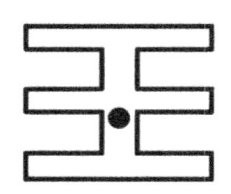

15.  Forward -

    walking stance (apsugi),

    high block (ulgul makki).

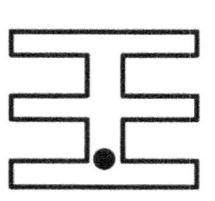

TAEGEUK YI JANG (2)

16 (Turn via left shoulder 270 degrees).

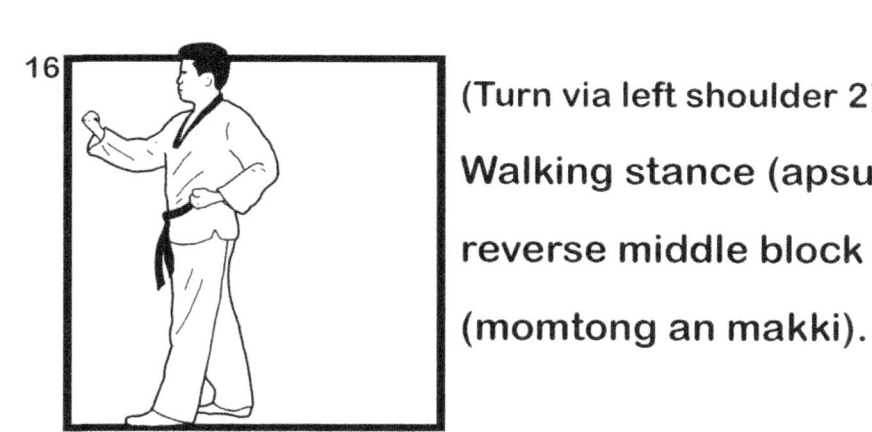

Walking stance (apsugi) reverse middle block (momtong an makki).

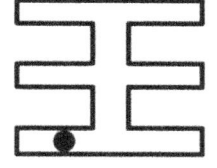

17  (Turn via left shoulder 180 degrees).

Walking stance (apsugi) reverse middle block (momtong an makki).

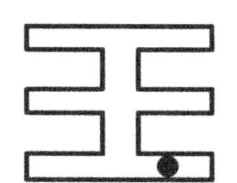

18  Backwards - (towards starting position) walking stance (apsugi) low block (areh makki).

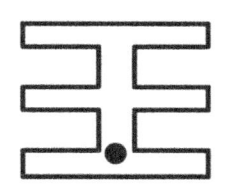

SIDE VIEW

19 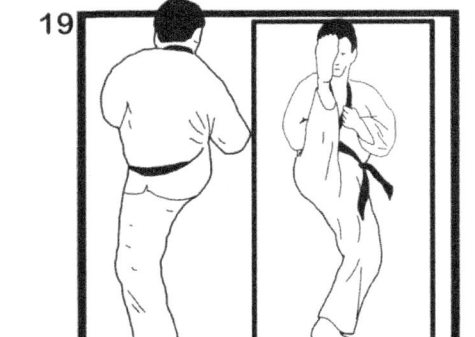 Front kick (apchuck ap chagi).

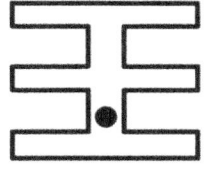

BACK VIEW

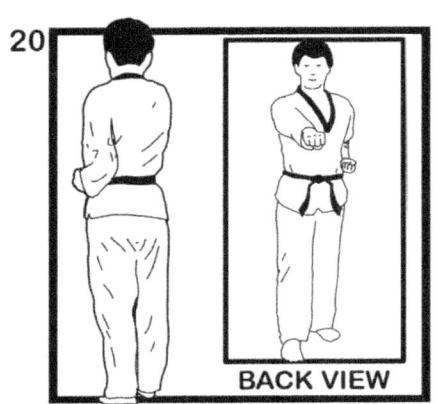

TAEGEUK YI JANG (2)

20. Walking stance (apsugi), middle punch (momtong bandai jireugi).

21. 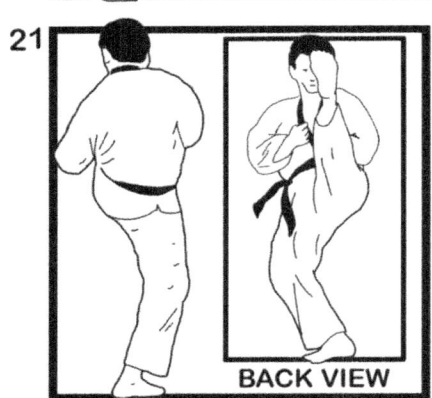 Front kick (apchuck ap chagi).

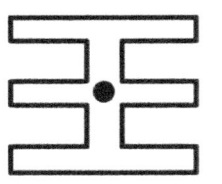

22. 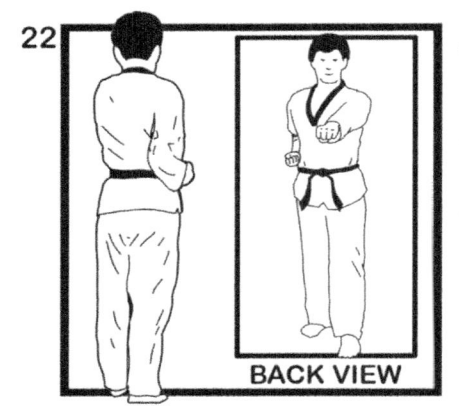 Walking stance (apsugi), middle punch (momtong bandai jireugi).

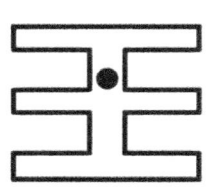

23. 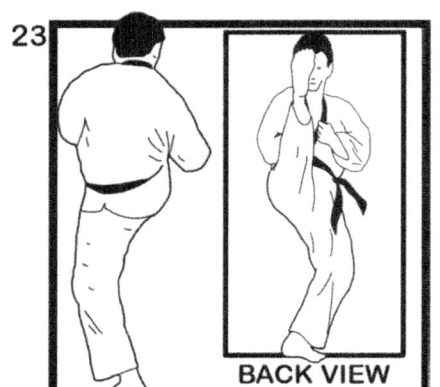 Front kick (apchuck ap chagi).

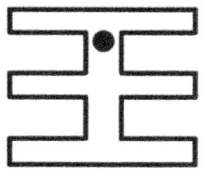

TAEGEUK YI JANG (2)

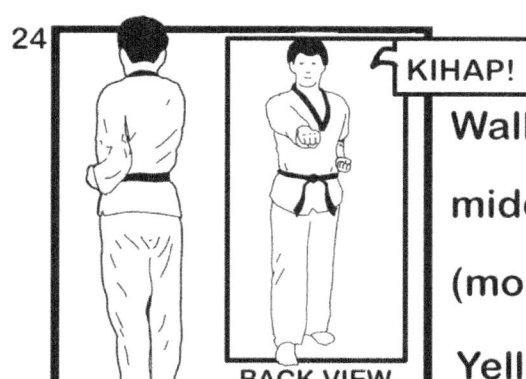

24. Walking stance (apsugi), middle punch (momtong bandai jireugi). Yell!

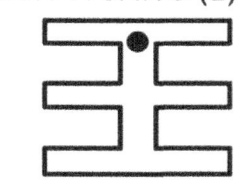

KIHAP!

BACK VIEW

25. Turn your left foot to ready stance (chonbi) legs parallel, hip width (naranhi sugi).

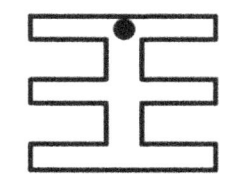

Taegeuk Form 3
(Taegeuk Sam Jang)

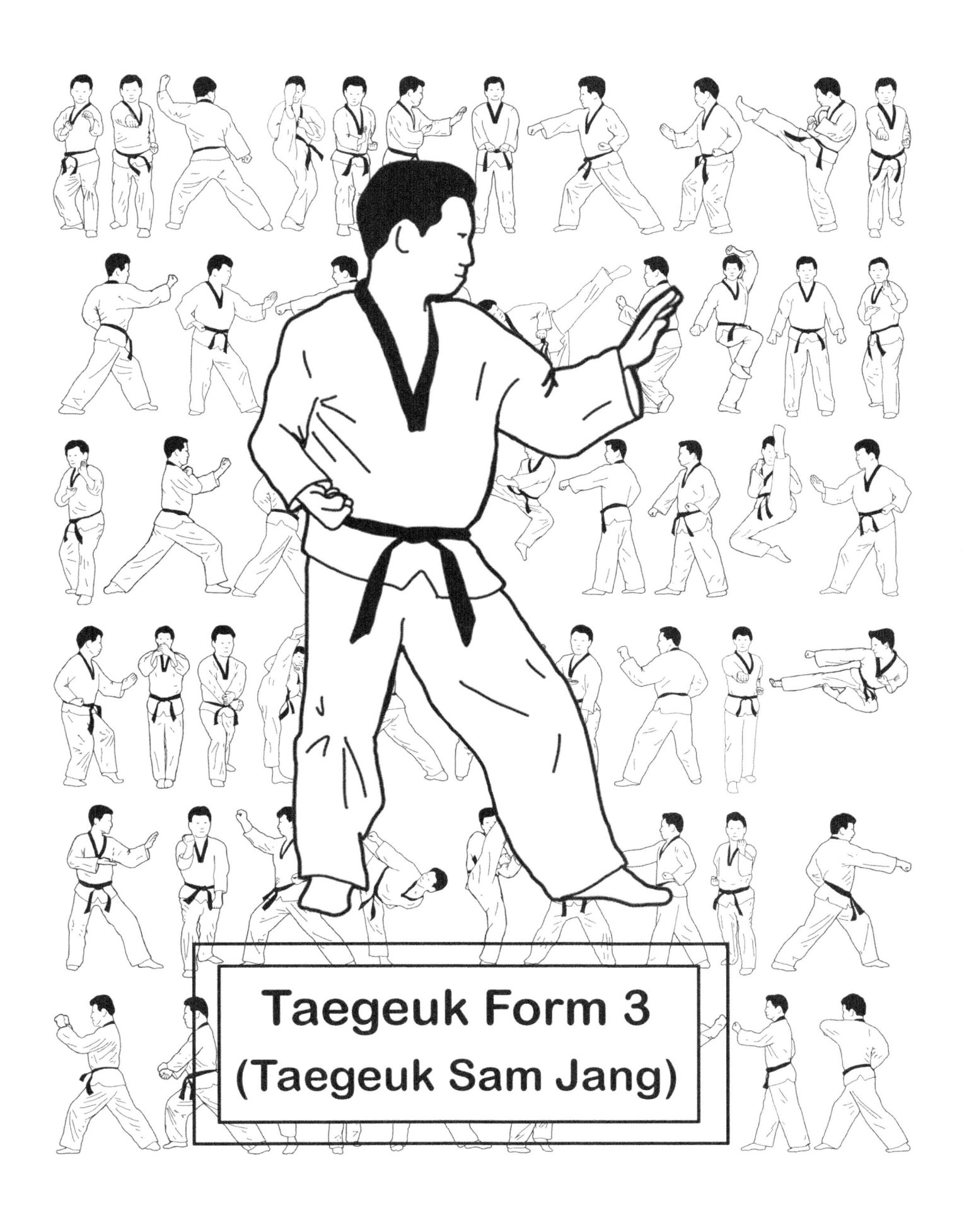

TAEGEUK SAM JANG (3)

TAEGEUK SAM JANG (3)

TAEGEUK SAM JANG (3) PART ONE

Ready stance

1. Walking stance, low block
2. Front kick
3A. Front stance, middle punch
3B. Front stance, reverse middle punch
4. Walking stance, low block
5. Front kick
6A. Front stance, middle punch
6B. Front stance, reverse middle punch 
7. Walking stance, reverse knife hand neck strike 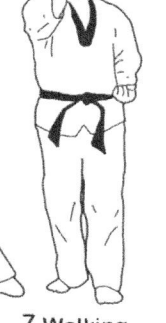
8. Walking stance, reverse knife hand neck strike 
9. Back stance, single knife-hand middle block 
10. Front stance, reverse middle punch 
11. Back stance, single knife-hand middle block 
12. Front stance, reverse middle punch 
13. Walking stance, reverse middle block 
14. Walking stance, reverse middle block

TAEGEUK SAM JANG (3) PART TWO

15. Walking stance, low block
16. Front kick
17A. Front stance, middle punch
17B. Front stance, reverse middle punch
18. Walking stance, low block
19. Front kick
20A. Front stance, middle punch
20B. Front stance, reverse middle punch
21. Walking stance, low block
22. Walking stance, reverse middle punch
23. Walking stance, low block
24. Walking stance, reverse middle punch
25. Front kick 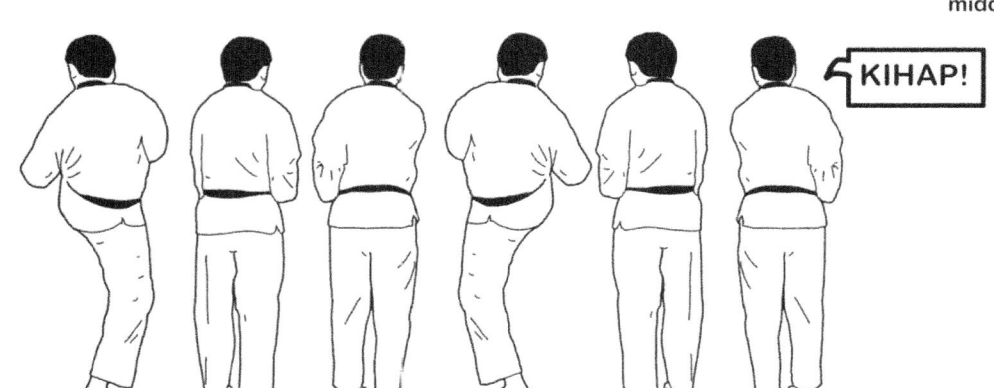
26. Walking stance, low block
27. Walking stance, reverse middle punch
28. Front kick
29. Walking stance, low block
30. Walking stance, reverse middle punch

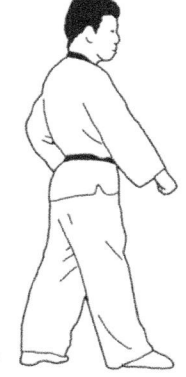

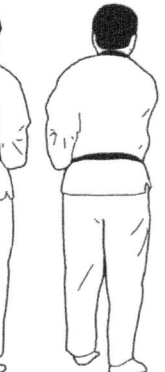

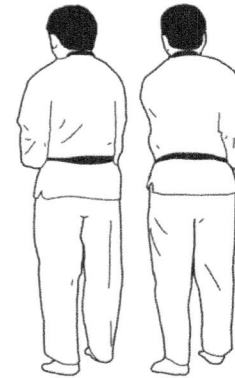

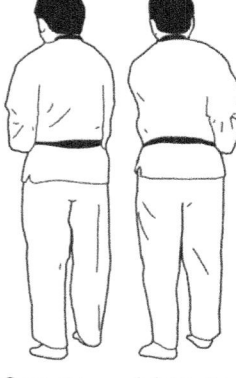

KIHAP!

Ready stance

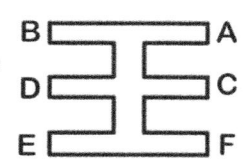

TAEGEUK SAM JANG (3)

Philosophical symbol is - Ri - signifying fire and sun.

This poomsae is a bit more complex and is suitable for green belts geup 6 and up. In addition to the basic techniques (as we have in the first and second poomsae) this poomsae also has a double punch, a back stance and attacks with open hands. We can see how the idea of fire is expressed in the poomsae, very strong and fast techniques as appear in the double punch.

1. Ready stance (chonbi) legs parallel, hip width (naranhi sugi).

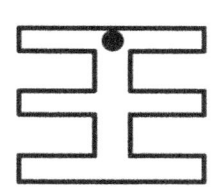

2. To your left - walking stance (apsugi), low block (arehmakki). Keep the block about a fist above the leg.

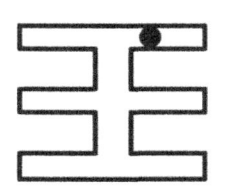

3. Front kick (apchuck ap chagi).

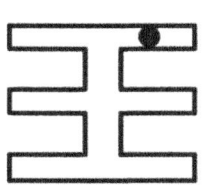

TAEGEUK SAM JANG (3)

4. Front stance (apkubi),

 middle punch

 (momtong bandai jireugi).

 Keep the punch aimed at the solar plexus.

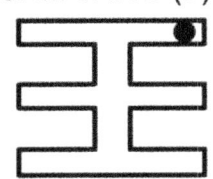

5.  Front stance (apkubi),

 reverse middle punch

 (momtong baro jireugi).

 Keep the punch aimed at the solar plexus.

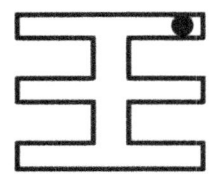

6.  To your right - walking stance

 (apsugi), low block (arehmakki).

 Keep the block about a fist

 above the leg.

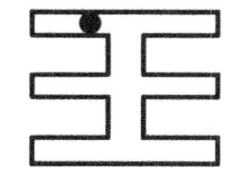

7.  Front kick (apchuck ap chagi).

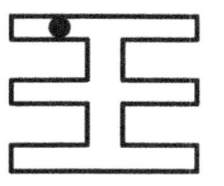

TAEGEUK SAM JANG (3)

8. Front stance (apkubi), middle punch (momtong bandai jireugi). Keep the punch aimed at the solar plexus.

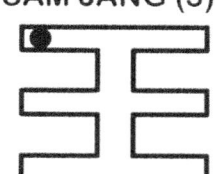

9.  Front stance (apkubi), reverse middle punch (momtong baro jireugi). Keep the punch aimed at the solar plexus.

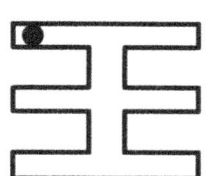

10. 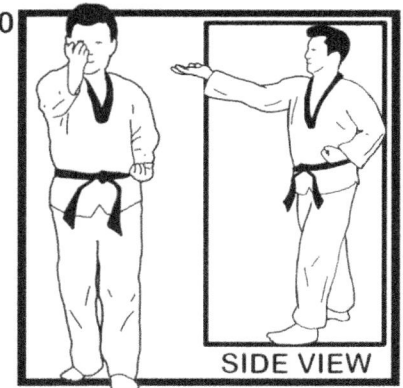 Forward - walking stance (apsugi), knife-hand neck strike (hansonal mok chigi).

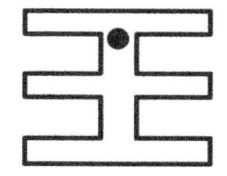

11.  Forward - walking stance (apsugi), knife-hand neck strike (hansonal mok chigi).

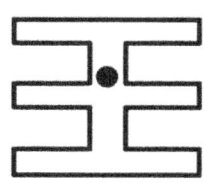

TAEGEUK SAM JANG (3)

12 To your left -

back stance (dwit kubi),

single knife-hand middle block

(hansonal momtong makki).

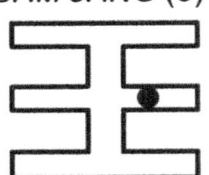

13  Shift to front stance (apkubi),

reverse middle punch

(momtong baro jireugi).

Keep the punch aimed at the solar plexus.

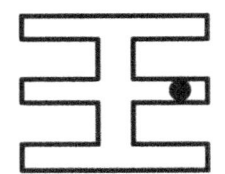

14  To your right -

back stance (dwit kubi),

single knife-hand middle block

(hansonal momtong makki).

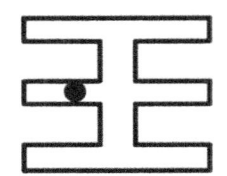

15  Shift to front stance (apkubi),

reverse middle punch

(momtong baro jireugi).

Keep the punch aimed at the solar plexus.

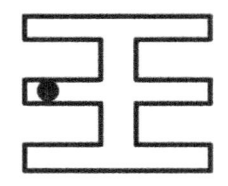

TAEGEUK SAM JANG (3)

16. Forward - walking stance (apsugi), reverse middle block (momtong an makki).

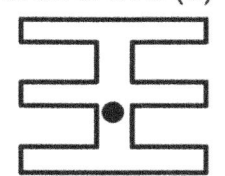

17. 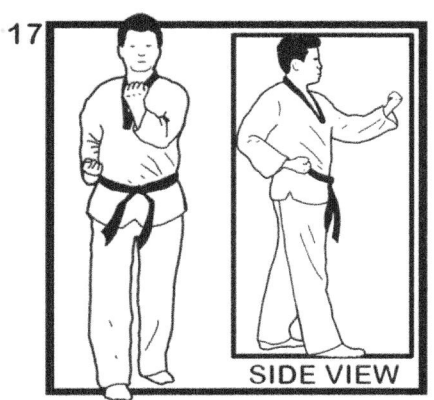 Forward - walking stance (apsugi), reverse middle block (momtong an makki).

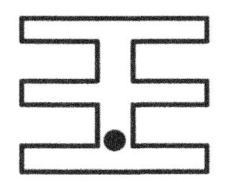

18.  (Turn via left shoulder 270 degrees). Walking stance (apsugi), low block (arehmakki). Keep the block about a fist above the leg.

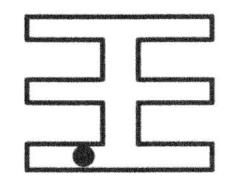

19.  Front kick (apchuck ap chagi).

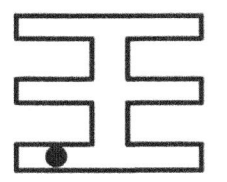

TAEGEUK SAM JANG (3)

20 Front stance (apkubi), middle punch (momtong bandai jireugi).

Keep the punch aimed at the solar plexus.

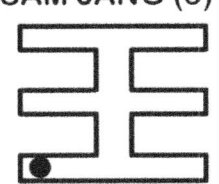

21  Front stance (apkubi), reverse middle punch (momtong baro jireugi).

Keep the punch aimed at the solar plexus.

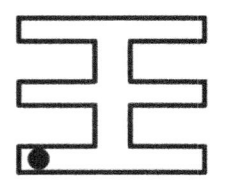

22  (Turn via right shoulder 180 degrees).

Walking stance (apsugi), low block (arehmakki).

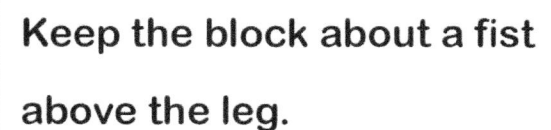

Keep the block about a fist above the leg.

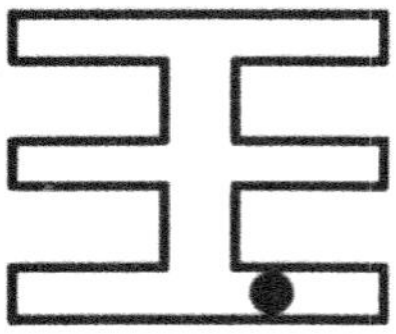

23 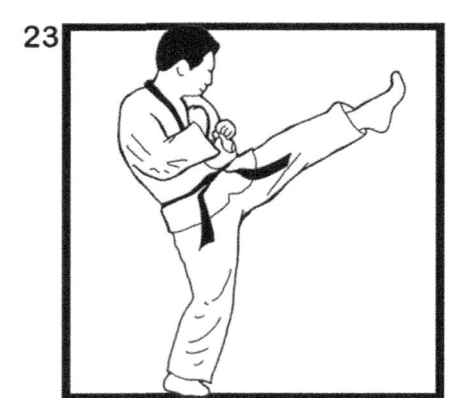 Front kick (apchuck ap chagi).

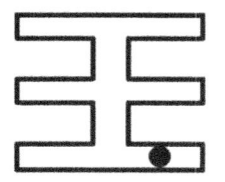

TAEGEUK SAM JANG (3)

24. Front stance (apkubi), middle punch (momtong bandai jireugi).

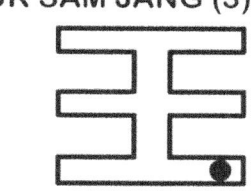

Keep the punch aimed at the solar plexus.

25. Front stance (apkubi), reverse middle punch (momtong baro jireugi).

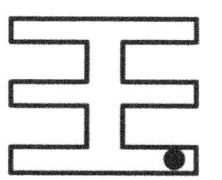

Keep the punch aimed at the solar plexus.

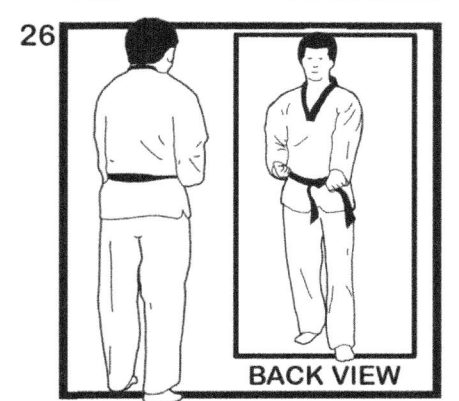

26. Backwards - (towards starting position) walking stance (apsugi), low block (areh makki).

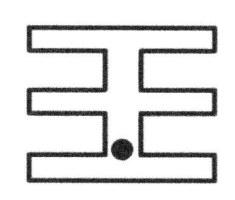

BACK VIEW

27. Walking stance (apsugi), reverse middle punch (momtong baro jireugi).

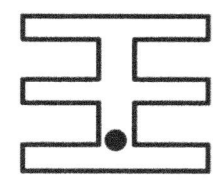

BACK VIEW

TAEGEUK SAM JANG (3)

28. Walking stance (apsugi), low block (areh makki).

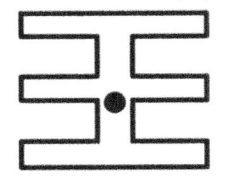

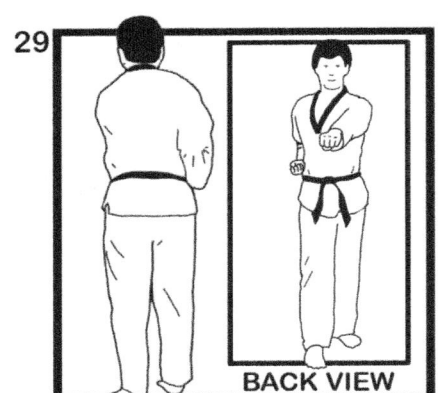

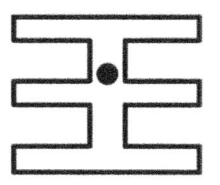

29. Walking stance (apsugi), reverse middle punch (momtong baro jireugi).

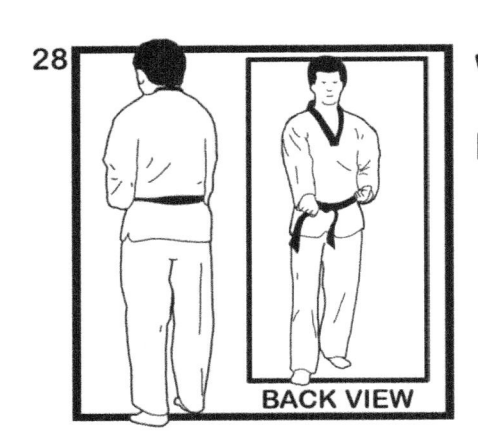

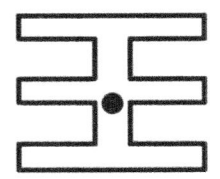

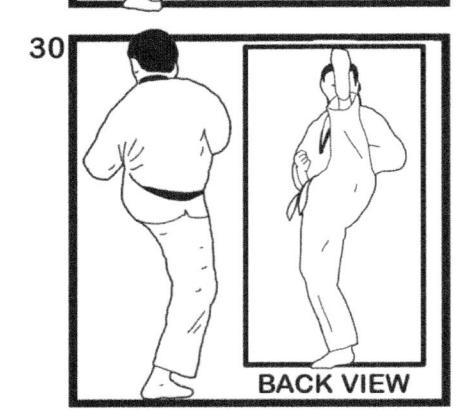

30. Front kick (apchuck ap chagi).

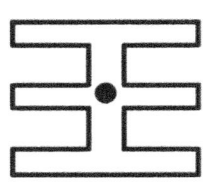

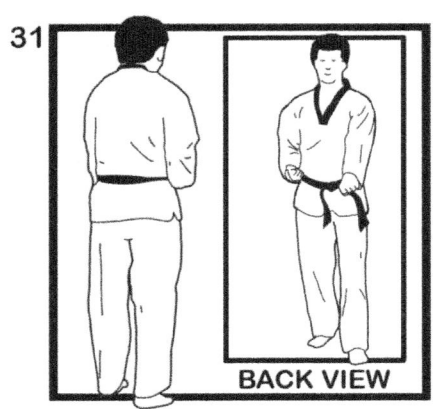

31. Walking stance (apsugi), low block (areh makki).

TAEGEUK SAM JANG (3)

32. Walking stance (apsugi), reverse middle punch (momtong baro jireugi).

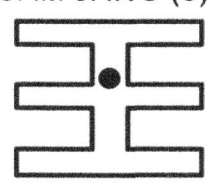

33. 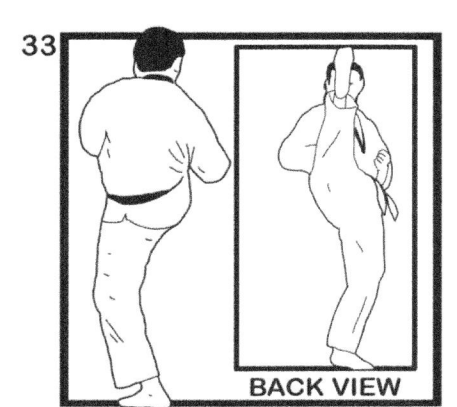 Front kick (apchuck ap chagi).

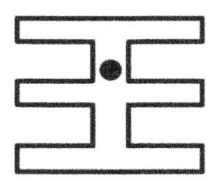

34. 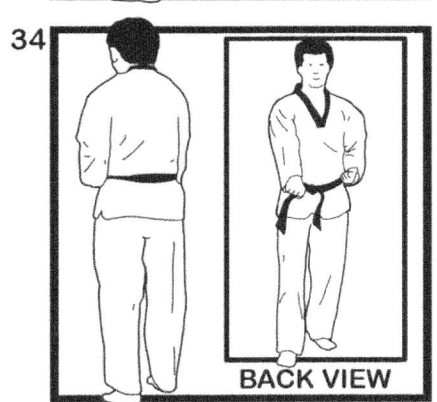 Walking stance (apsugi), low block (areh makki).

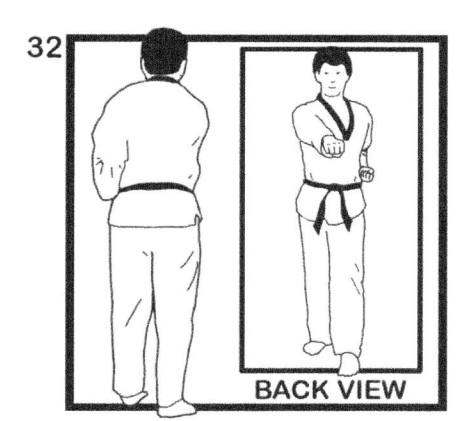

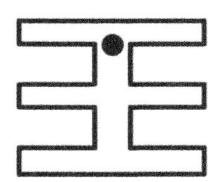

35.  KIHAP! Walking stance (apsugi), reverse middle punch (momtong baro jireugi). Yell!

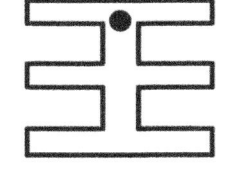

47

TAEGEUK SAM JANG (3)

36 Turn your left foot to ready stance (chonbi) legs parallel, hip width (naranhi sugi).

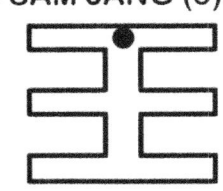

Taegeuk Form 4 (Taegeuk Sa Jang)

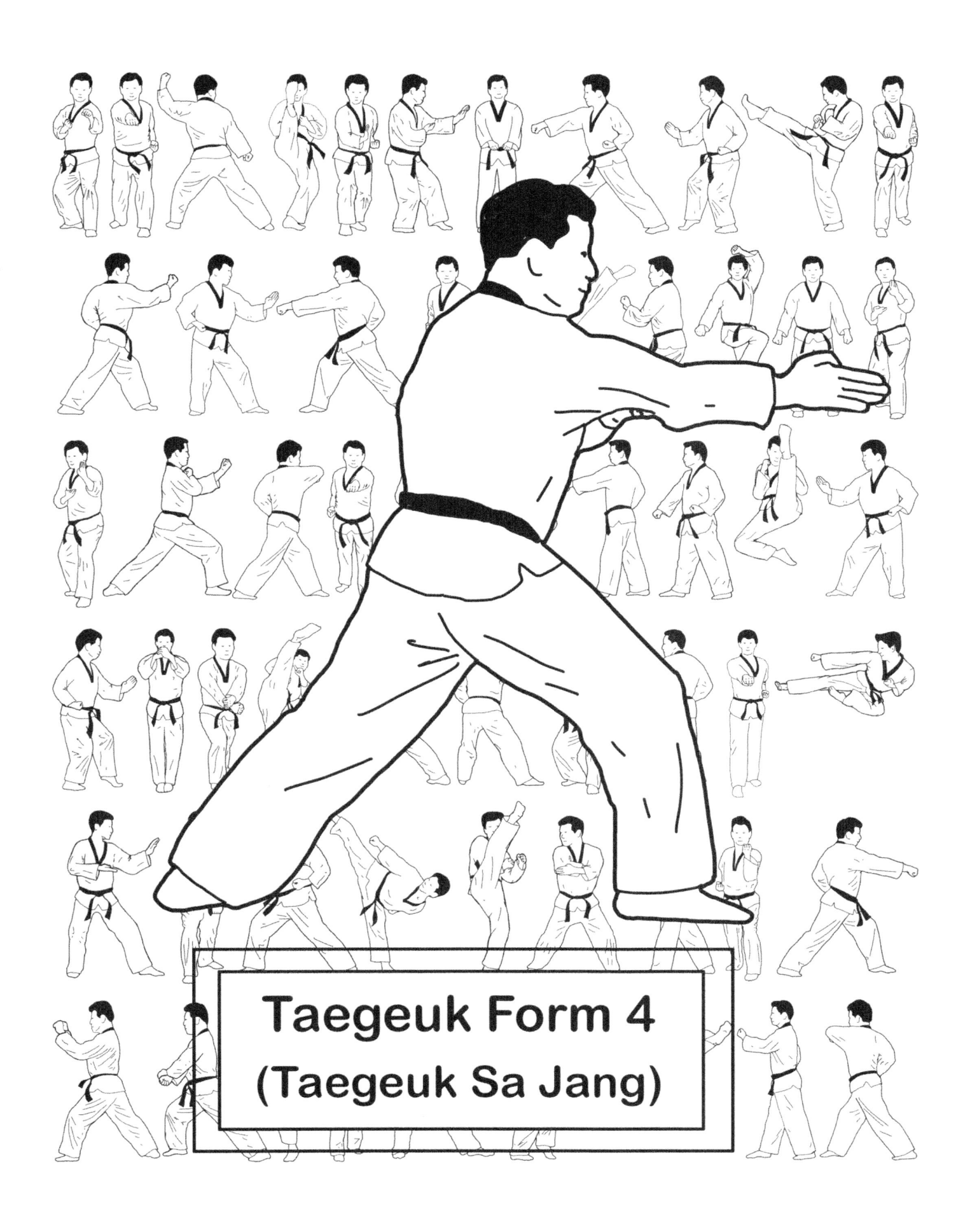

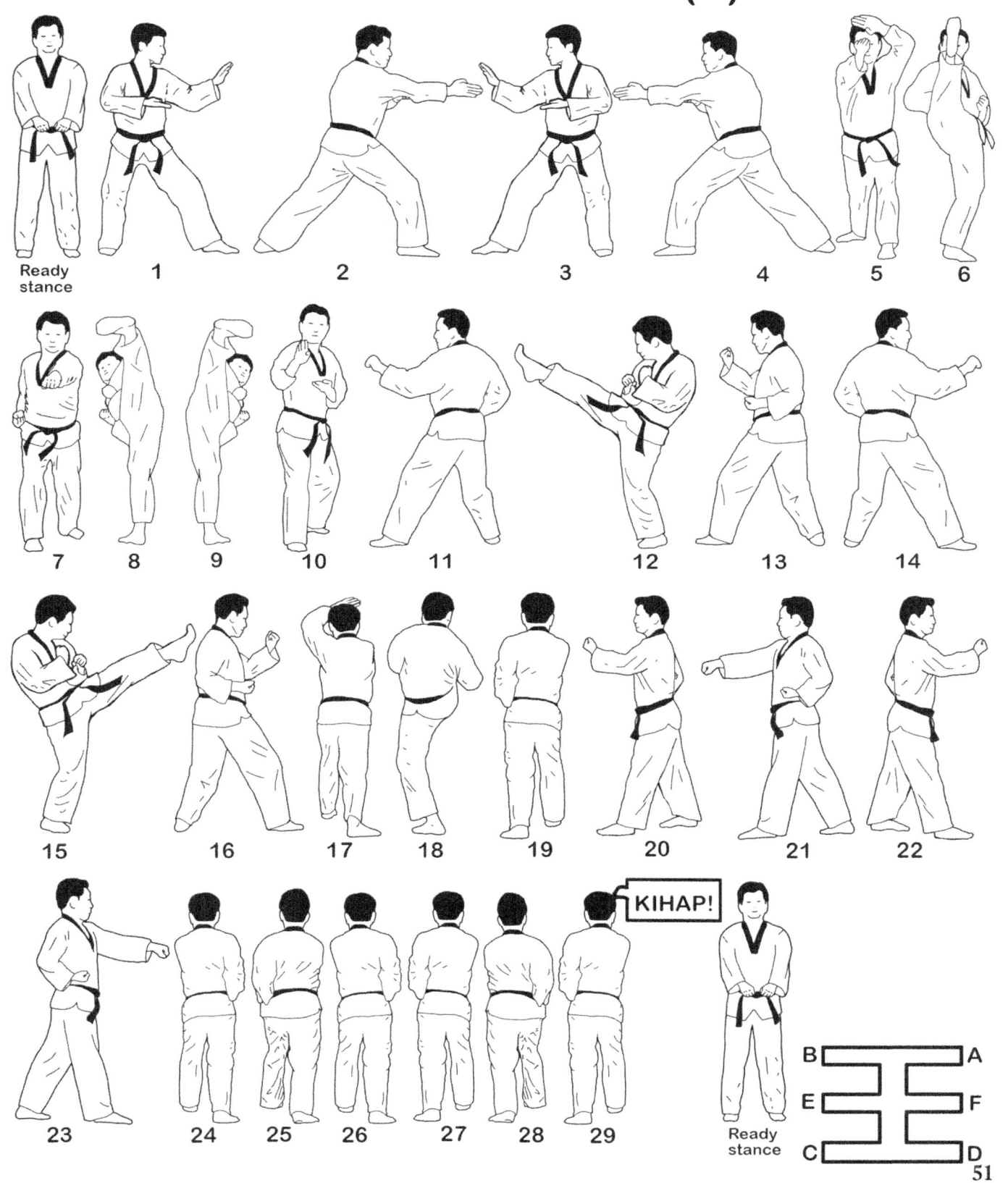

TAEGEUK SA JANG (4)

TAEGEUK SA JANG (4)

TAEGEUK SA JANG (4) PART ONE

1. Ready stance
2. Back stance knife hand middle outward block
3. Front stance spear hand strike
4. Back stance knife hand middle outward block
5. Front stance spear hand strike
6. Front stance, swallow shape knife-hand neck strike
7. Front kick
8. Front stance, reverse middle punch
9. Side kick
10. Side kick
11. Back stance, knife hand middle outward block
12. Back stance, middle outward block
13. Front kick
14. Back stance, inward middle block
15. Back stance, outward middle block
16. Front kick
17. Back stance, inward middle block

TAEGEUK SA JANG (4) PART TWO

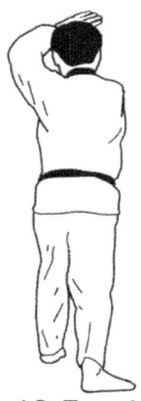

18. Front stance, swallow shape knife-hand neck strike 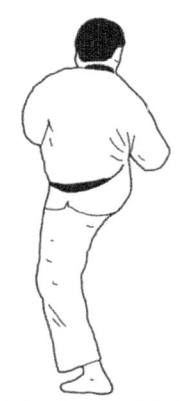
19. Front kick 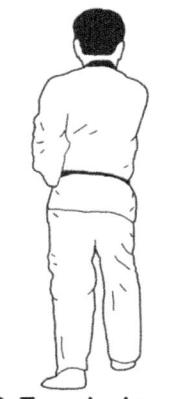
20. Front stance, back fist 
21. Walking stance, middle block 
22. Walking stance, middle reverse punch 
23. Walking stance, middle block 
24. Walking stance, middle reverse punch 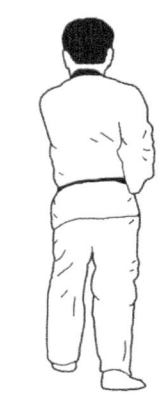
25. Front stance, middle block 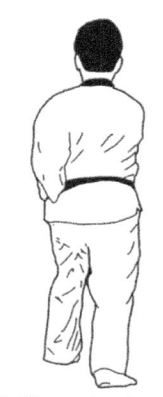
26. Front stance, reverse middle punch 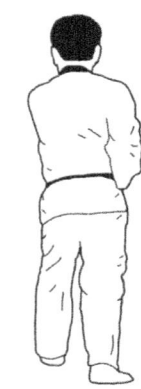
27. Front stance, middle punch 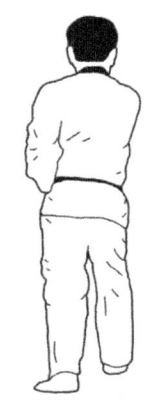
28. Front stance, middle block 
29. Front stance, reverse middle punch 
30. Front stance, middle punch 
31. Ready stance

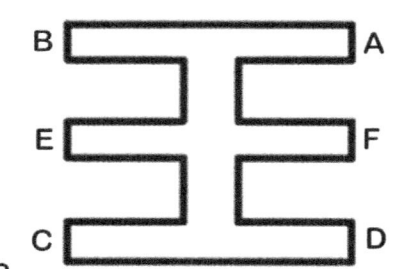

KIHAP!

```
B ─────        ───── A
        │    │
E ──────┤    ├───── F
        │    │
C ─────        ───── D
```

54

TAEGEUK SA JANG (4)

Philosophical meaning is - Gin - meaning thunder and lightning.
Thunder and lightning create fear in people's hearts, they should be brave in the face of danger. This poomsae has advanced and sophisticated techniques and is suitable to purple belts, geup 5 and up. This poomsae has swallow's thrust, knife hand block, side kicks and more. You can see how the idea of thunder and lightning can be expressed in this form due to the strong hand strikes with an open hand, and the spear hand strike.

1. Ready stance (chonbi) legs parallel, hip width (naranhi sugi).

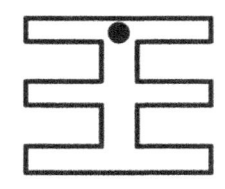

2.  To your left - back stance (dwit kubi), knife-hand middle outward block (sonal momtong makki).

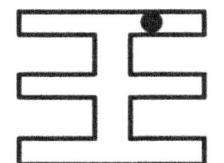

3.  Front stance (apkubi), spear hand strike (pyong sonkut jireugi).
Some Taekwondo clubs do palm hand downward block here (batangson nelyo makki), before the strike, or with the strike.

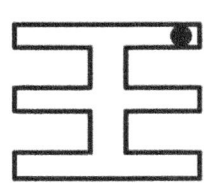

TAEGEUK SA JANG (4)

4.  To your right - back stance (dwit kubi), knife-hand middle outward block (sonal momtong makki).

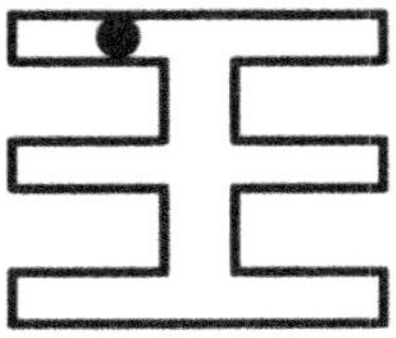

5.  Front stance (ap kubi), spear hand strike (pyong sonkut jireugi).
Some Taekwondo clubs do palm hand downward block here (batangson nelyo makki), before the strike, or with the strike. 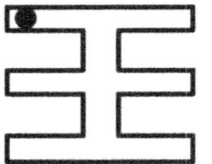

6.  Forward - front stance (ap kubi), swallow shape knife-hand neck strike (jebipoom mok chigi).

SIDE VIEW

7. 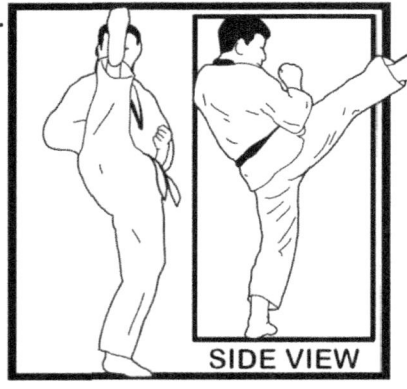 Front kick (apchuck ap chagi).

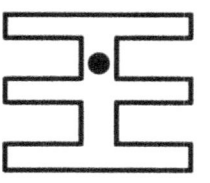

SIDE VIEW

TAEGEUK SA JANG (4)

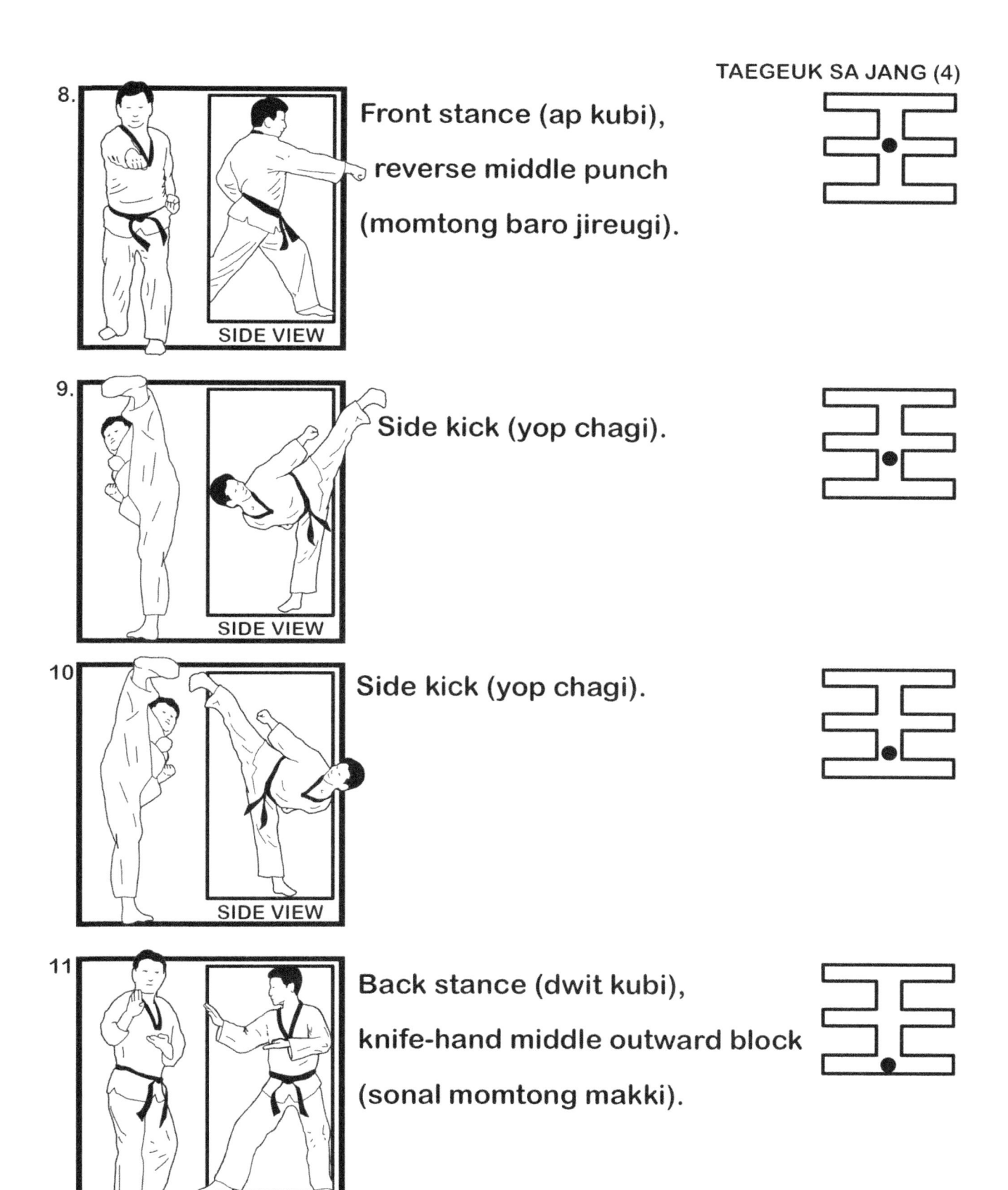

8. Front stance (ap kubi), reverse middle punch (momtong baro jireugi).

9. Side kick (yop chagi).

10. Side kick (yop chagi).

11. Back stance (dwit kubi), knife-hand middle outward block (sonal momtong makki).

TAEGEUK SA JANG (4)

12 (Turn via left shoulder 270 degrees).

Back stance (dwit kubi),

middle outward block

(momtong bakat makki).

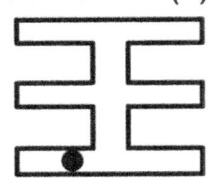

13  Front kick

(apchuck ap chagi).

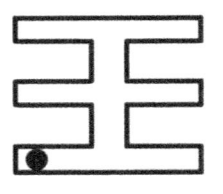

14  Back stance (dwit kubi),

reverse middle block

from outside in

(momtong an makki).

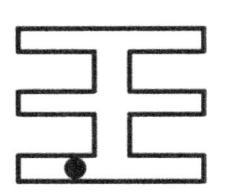

15  (Turn via right shoulder 180 degrees).

Back stance (dwit kubi),

middle outward block

(momtong bakat makki).

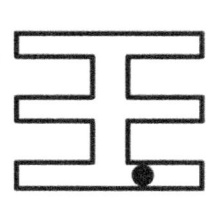

TAEGEUK SA JANG (4)

16. Front kick (apchuck ap chagi).

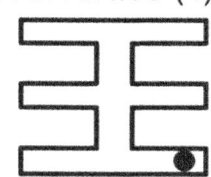

17.  Back stance (dwit kubi), with reverse middle block from outside in (momtong an makki).

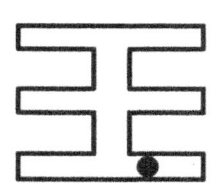

18.  Backward - (towards starting position) front stance (apkubi), swallow shape knife-hand neck strike (jebipoom mok chigi).

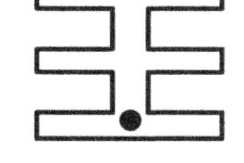

SIDE VIEW

19.  Front kick (apchuck ap chagi).

SIDE VIEW

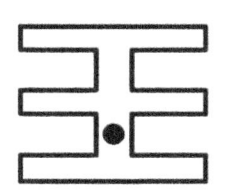

TAEGEUK SA JANG (4)

20. Front stance (apkubi), back fist front strike (dong jumeok apachigi).

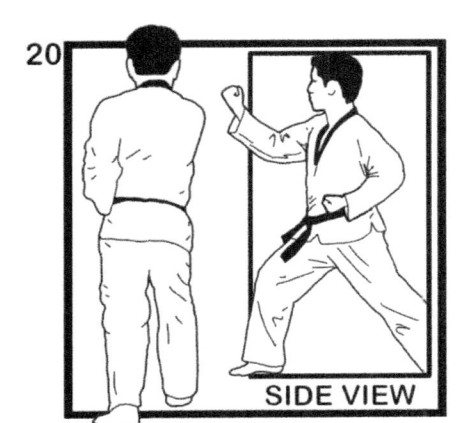

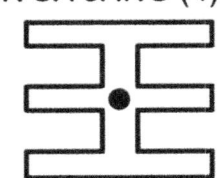

21.  To your left – walking stance (apsugi), middle block from outside in (momtong makki).

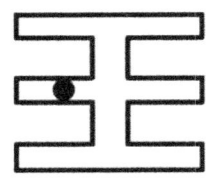

22.  Walking stance (apsugi), with reverse middle punch (momtong baro jireugi).

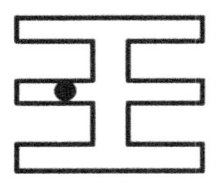

23.  (Turn via right shoulder 180 degrees). Walking stance (apsugi), middle block from outside in (momtong makki).

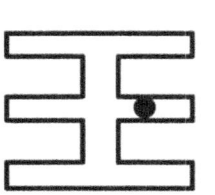

TAEGEUK SA JANG (4)

24. Walking stance (apsugi), reverse middle punch (momtong baro jireugi).

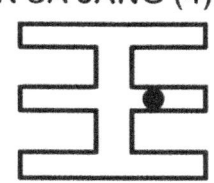

25. 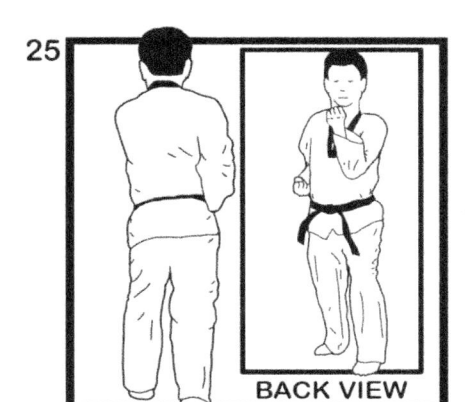 Backward - (towards starting position) front stance (apkubi), middle block from outside in (momtong makki).

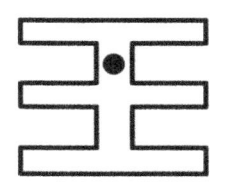

26.  Front stance (apkubi), reverse middle punch (momtong baro jireugi).

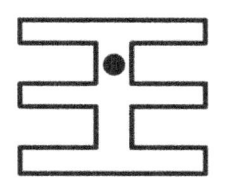

27. 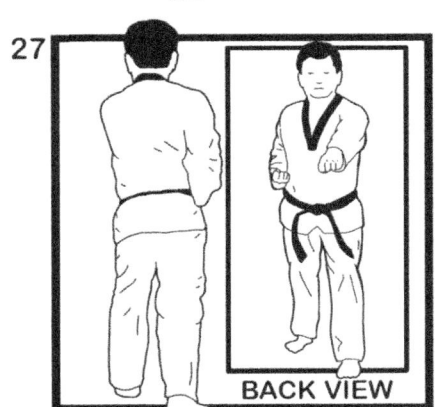 Front stance (apkubi), middle punch (momtong bandai jireugi).

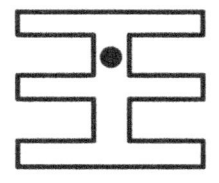

61

TAEGEUK SA JANG (4)

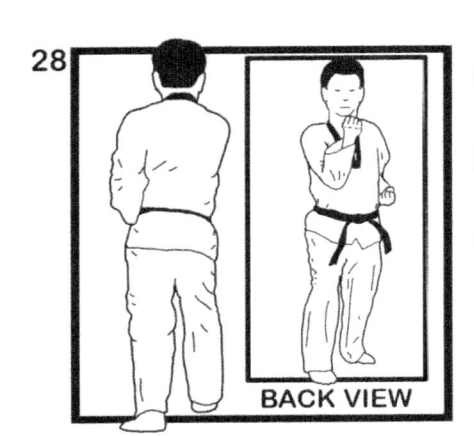

28. Front stance (apkubi), middle block from outside in (momtong makki).

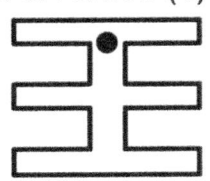

29. 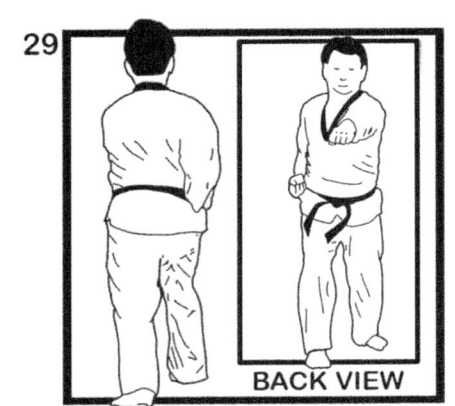 Front stance (apkubi), reverse middle punch (momtong baro jireugi).

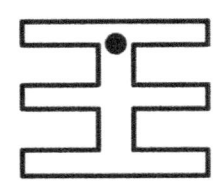

30.  KIHAP! Front stance (apkubi), middle punch (momtong bandai jireugi). Yell!

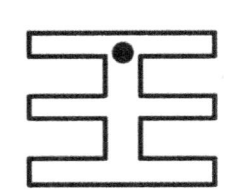

31.  Turn your left foot to ready stance (chonbi) legs parallel, hip width (naranhi sugi).

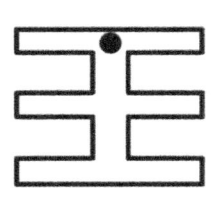

Taegeuk Form 5
(Taegeuk Oh Jang)

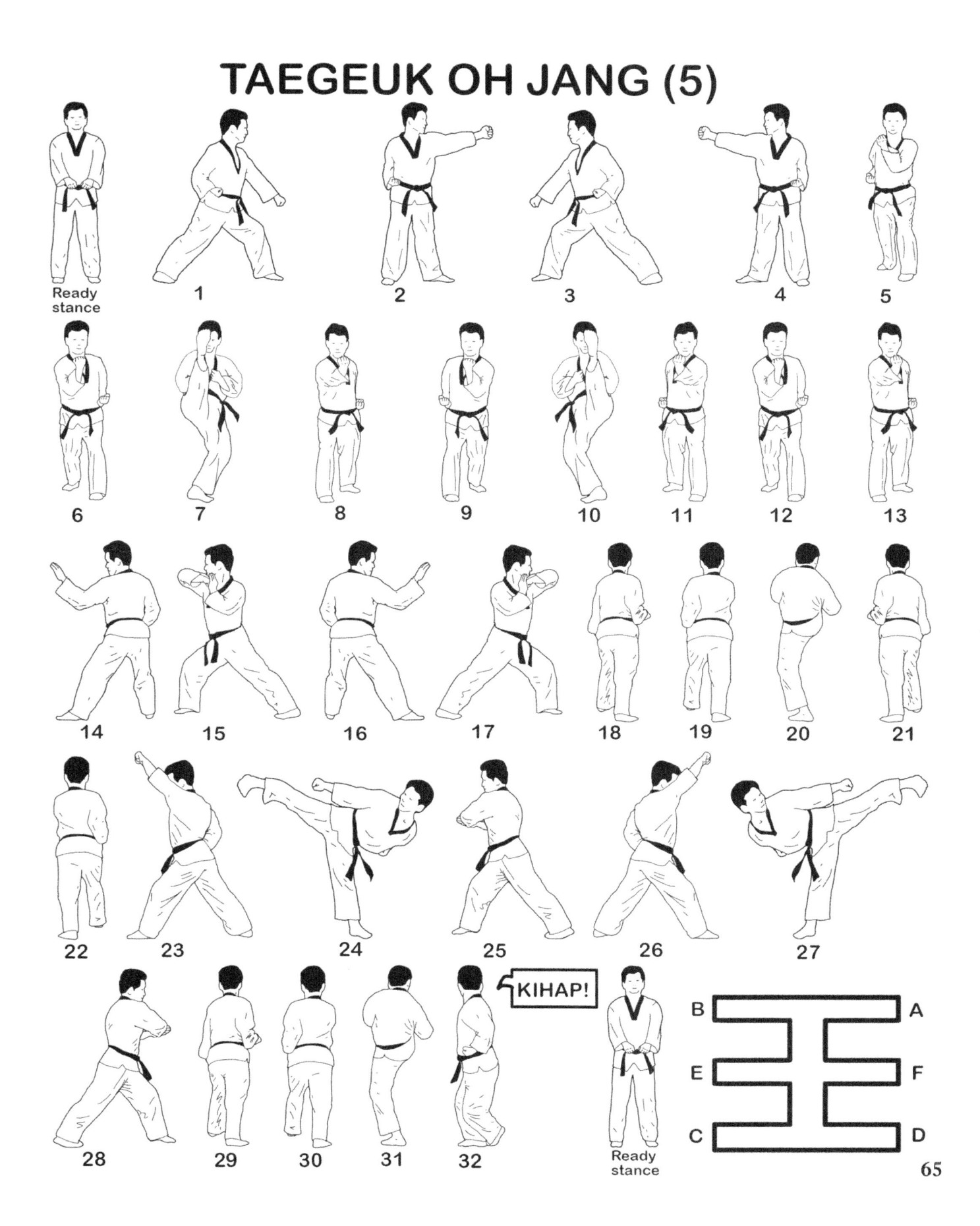

TAEGEUK OH JANG (5)

TAEGEUK OH JANG (5)

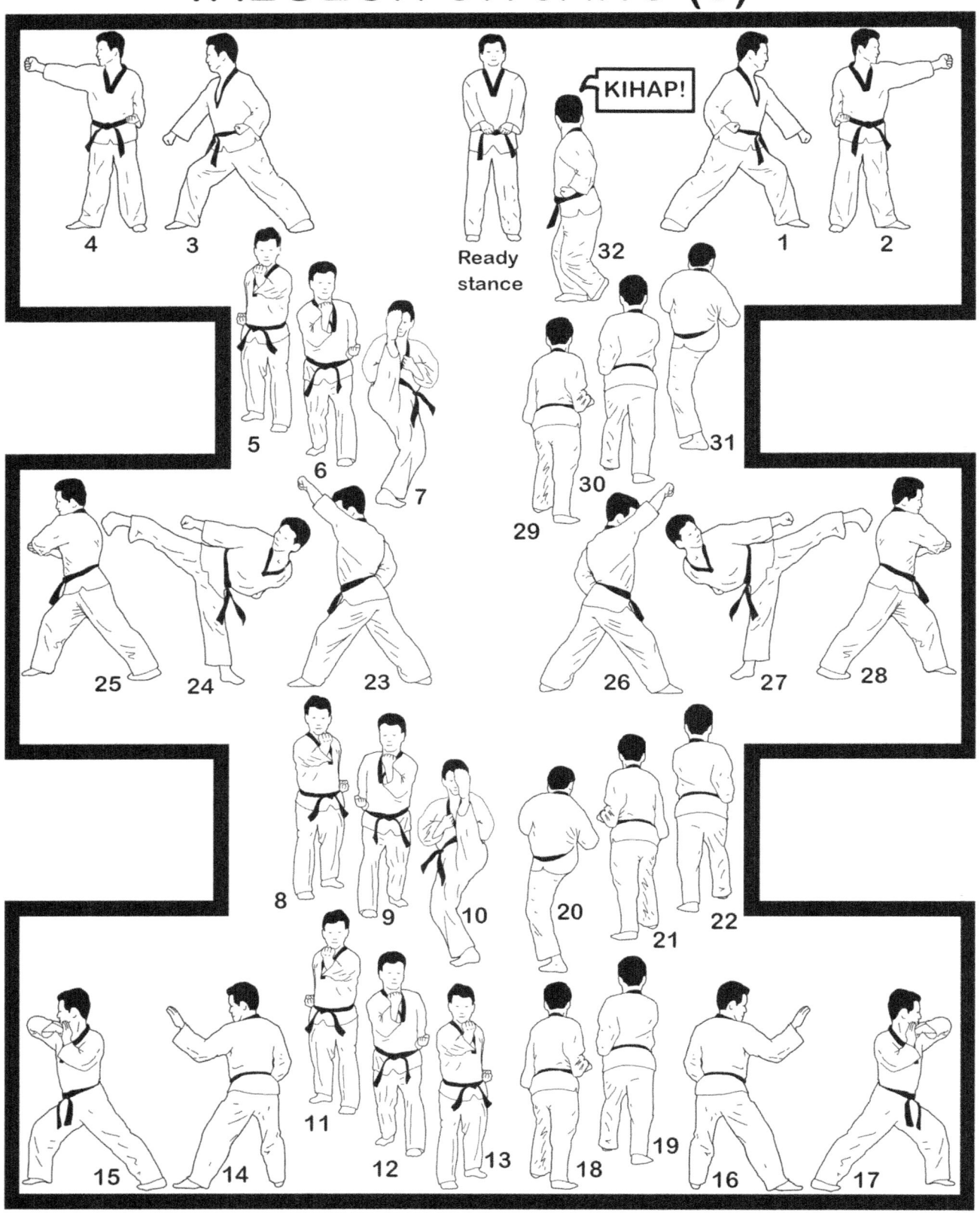

TAEGEUK OH JANG (5) PART ONE

1. Ready stance
2. Front stance, low block
3. Left stance, hammer fist
4. Front stance, low block 
5. Right stance, hammer fist
6. Front stance, middle block
7. Front stance, reverse middle block 
8. Front kick 
9. Front stance, back fist front strike 
10. Front stance, reverse middle block 
11. Front kick 
12. Front stance, back fist front strike 
13. Front stance, reverse middle block 
14. Front stance, back fist front strike 
15. Back stance, single knife hand middle block 
16. Front stance, elbow strike 
17. Back stance, single knife hand middle block 
18. Front stance, elbow strike 
19. Front stance, low block 
20. Front stance, reverse middle block

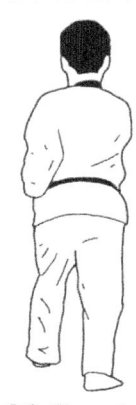

TAEGEUK OH JANG (5) PART TWO

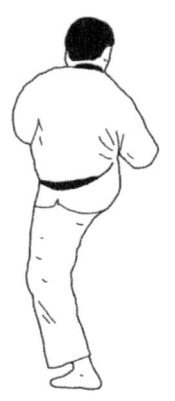

21. Front kick 
22. Front stance, low block 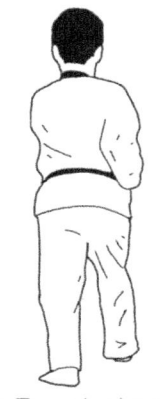
23. Front stance, reverse middle block
24. Front stance, high block
25. Side kick with side punch 
26. Front stance, elbow strike 
27. Front stance, high block
28. Side kick with side punch 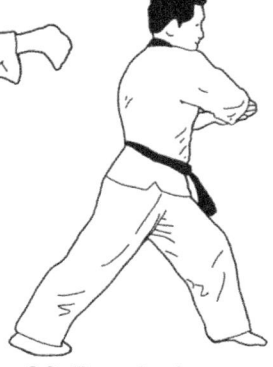
29. Front stance, elbow strike 
30. Front stance, low block 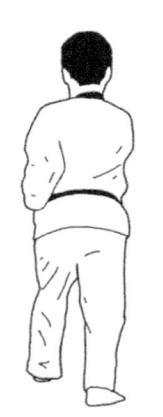
31. Front stance, reverse middle block 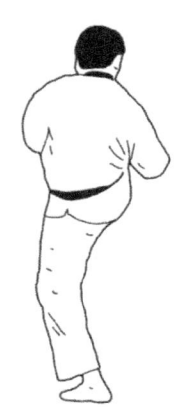
32. Front kick 
33. Cross stance, back fist front strike

KIHAP!

34. Ready stance

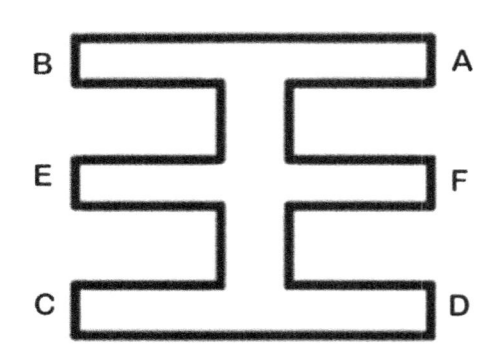

TAEGEUK OH JANG (5)

Philosophical meaning is - Seon - symbolizing wind, an invisible force. This is an advanced form for purple-blue belts, geup 4 and up. This poomsae has a few very strong and deadly attacks such as hammer fist strike, elbow strike, back fist strike and also complex techniques such as x-block.

1. Ready stance (chonbi) legs parallel, hip width (naranhi sugi).

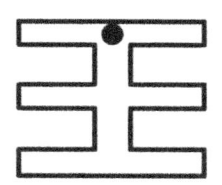

2.  To your left - front stance (apkubi), low block (areh makki).

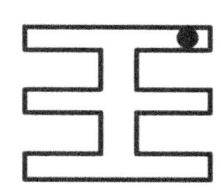

3.  Left stance (wen sugi), hammer fist downward strike (ma jumeok naeryo chigi).

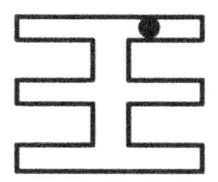

TAEGEUK OH JANG (5)

4. To your right -

   front stance (apkubi),

   low block (areh makki).

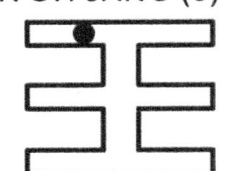

5. Right stance (oreun sugi),

   hammer fist downward strike

   (ma jumeok naeryo chigi).

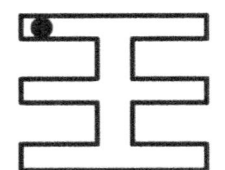

6. Forward -

   front stance (apkubi),

   middle block from outside in

   (momtong makki).

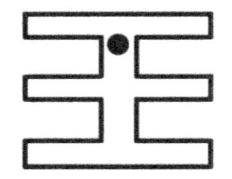

7. Front stance (apkubi),

   reverse middle block

   from outside in

   (momtong an makki).

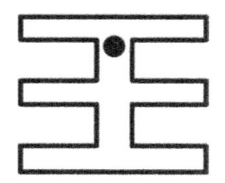

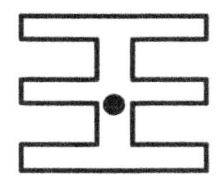

TAEGEUK OH JANG (5)

8. Front kick (apchuck ap chagi).

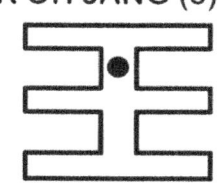

9. Front stance (apkubi), back fist front strike (dong jumeok apachigi).

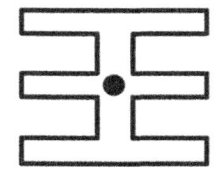

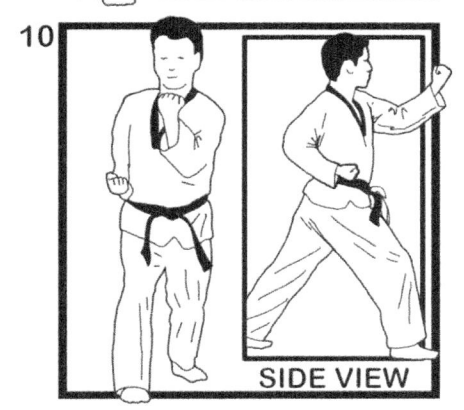

10. Front stance (apkubi), reverse middle block from outside in (momtong an makki).

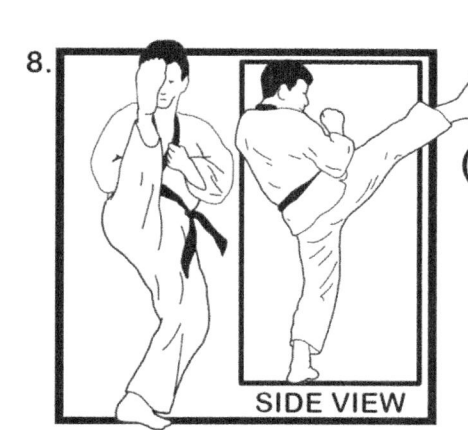

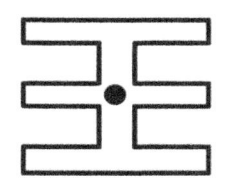

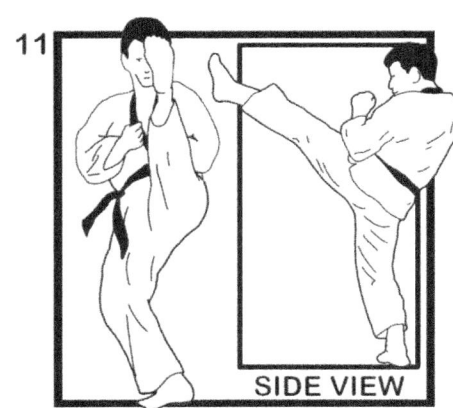

11. Front kick (apchuck ap chagi).

TAEGEUK OH JANG (5)

12. Front stance (apkubi), back fist front strike (dong jumeok apachigi).

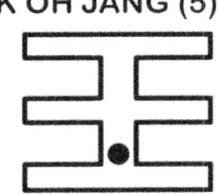

13. Front stance (apkubi), reverse middle block from outside in (momtong an makki).

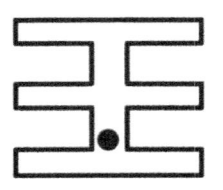

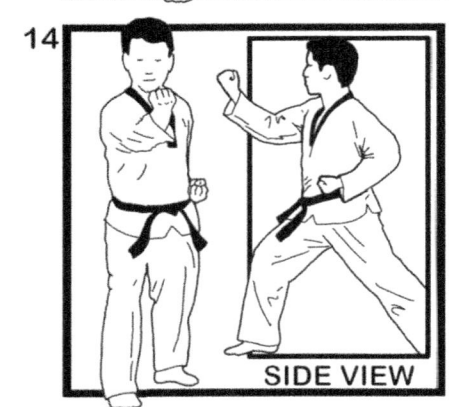

14. Front stance (apkubi), back fist front strike (dong jumeok apachigi).

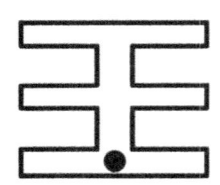

15. (Turn via left shoulder 270 degrees). Back stance (dwit kubi), single knife-hand middle block (hansonal momtong makki).

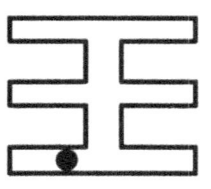

TAEGEUK OH JANG (5)

16. Front stance (apkubi), elbow strike (palkup chigi).

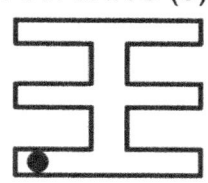

17.  (Turn via right shoulder 180 degrees). 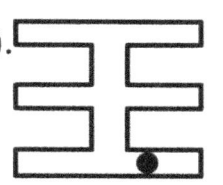 Back stance (dwit kubi), single knife-hand middle block (hansonal momtong makki).

18. Front stance (apkubi), elbow strike (palkup chigi).

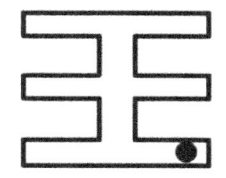

19. 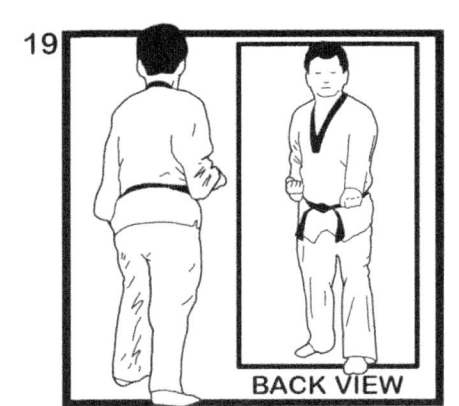 Backward - (towards starting position) front stance (apkubi), low block (areh makki).

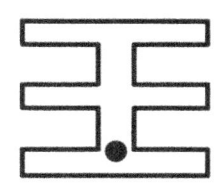

BACK VIEW

TAEGEUK OH JANG (5)

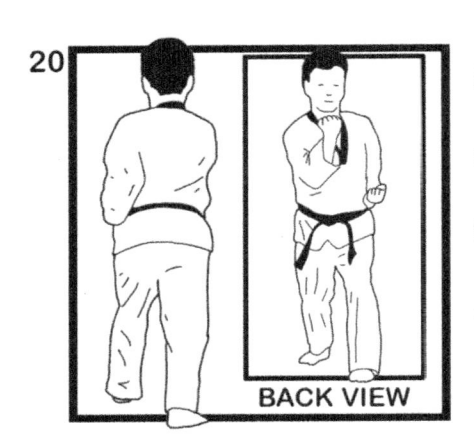

20. Front stance (apkubi), reverse middle block from outside in (momtong an makki).

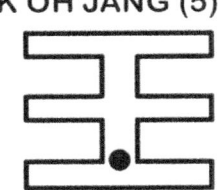

21. 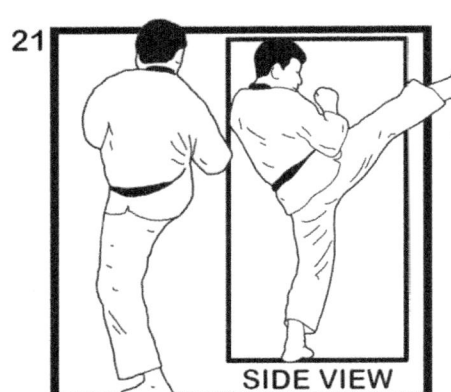 Front kick (apchuck ap chagi).

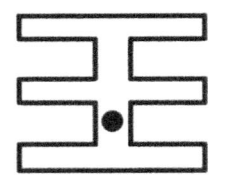

22.  Front stance (apkubi), low block (areh makki).

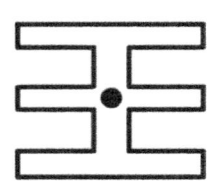

23. 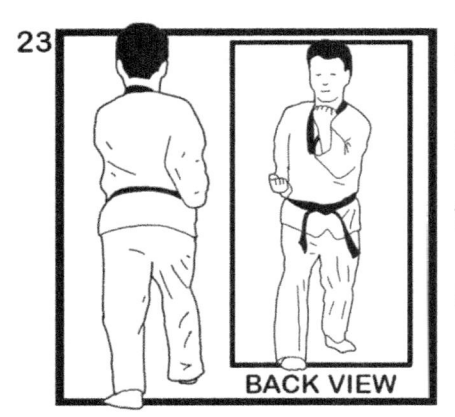 Front stance (apkubi), reverse middle block from outside in (momtong an makki).

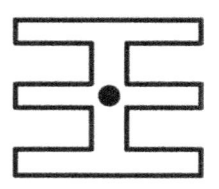

TAEGEUK OH JANG (5)

24 To your left –

front stance (apkubi),

high block (ulgul makki).

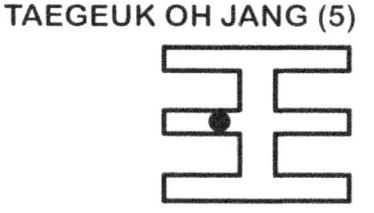

25 Side kick (yop chagi),

with side punch (yop jireugi)

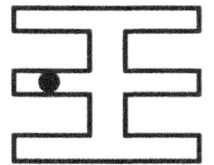

26 Front stance (apkubi),

left elbow strike

to the right palm

(palkup pyojeok chigi).

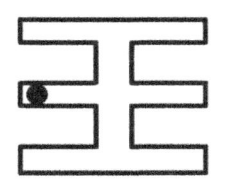

SIDE VIEW

27 (Turn via right shoulder 180 degrees).

Front stance (apkubi),

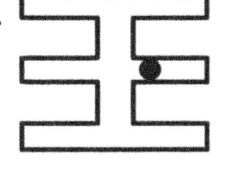

high block (ulgul makki).

TAEGEUK OH JANG (5)

28. Side kick (yop chagi), with side punch (yop jireugi).

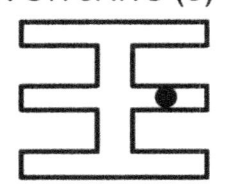

29. Front stance (apkubi), right elbow strike to the left palm (palkup pyojeok chigi).

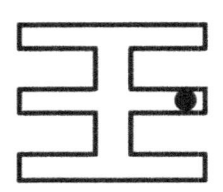

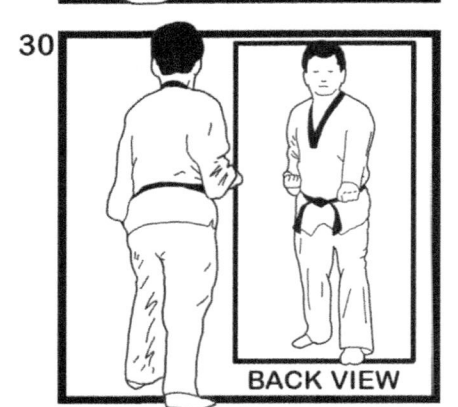

30. Backward - (towards starting position) front stance (apkubi), low block (areh makki).

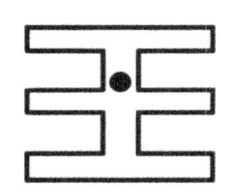

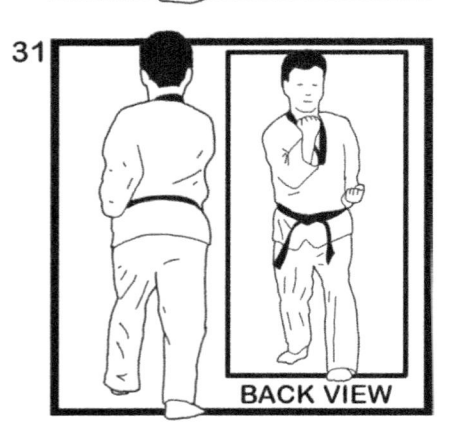

31. Front stance (apkubi), reverse middle block from outside in (momtong an makki).

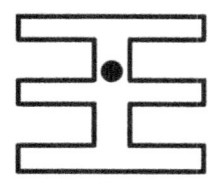

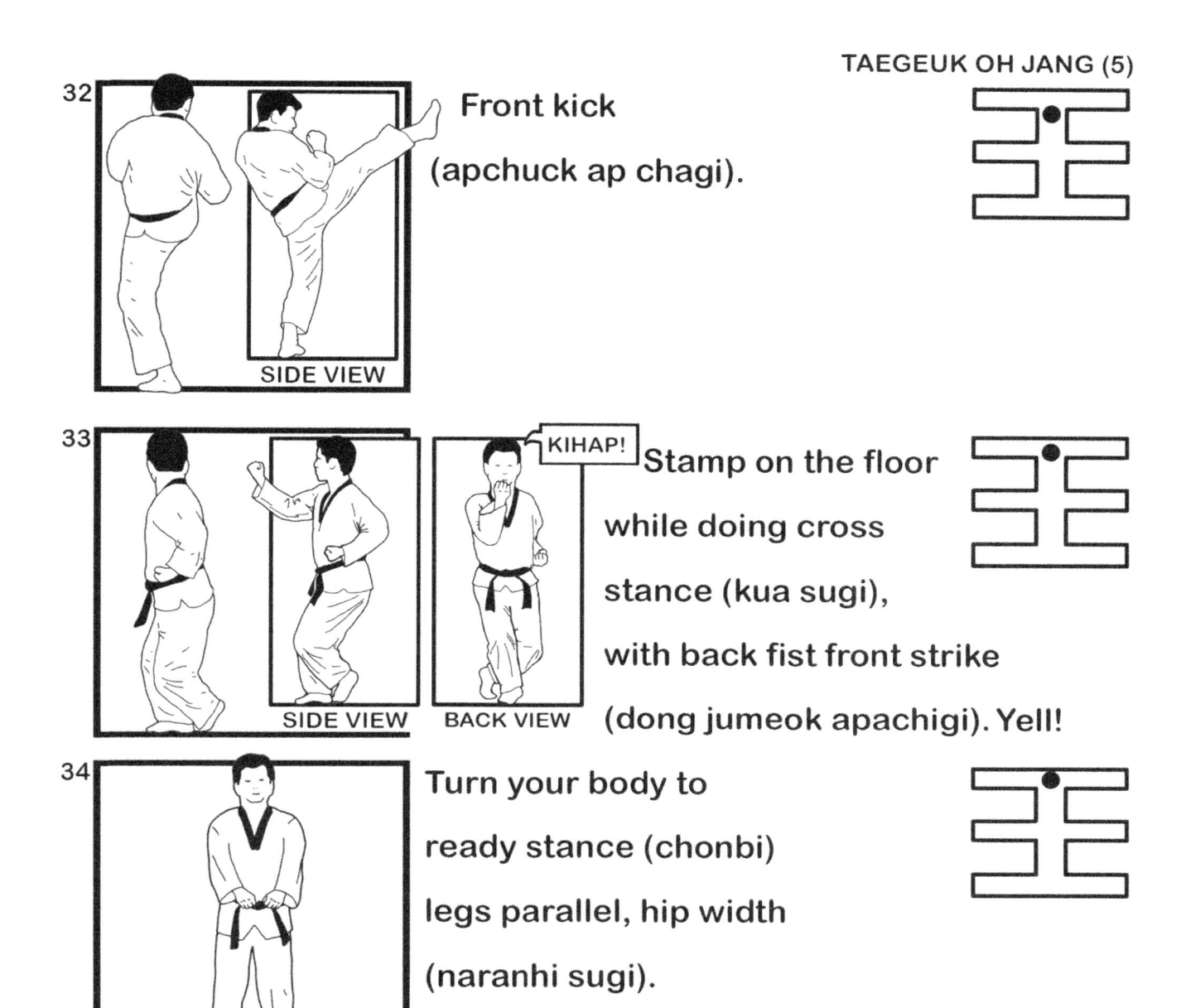

TAEGEUK OH JANG (5)

32. Front kick (apchuck ap chagi).

33. Stamp on the floor while doing cross stance (kua sugi), with back fist front strike (dong jumeok apachigi). Yell!

34. Turn your body to ready stance (chonbi) legs parallel, hip width (naranhi sugi).

Taegeuk Form 6
(Taegeuk Yuk Jang)

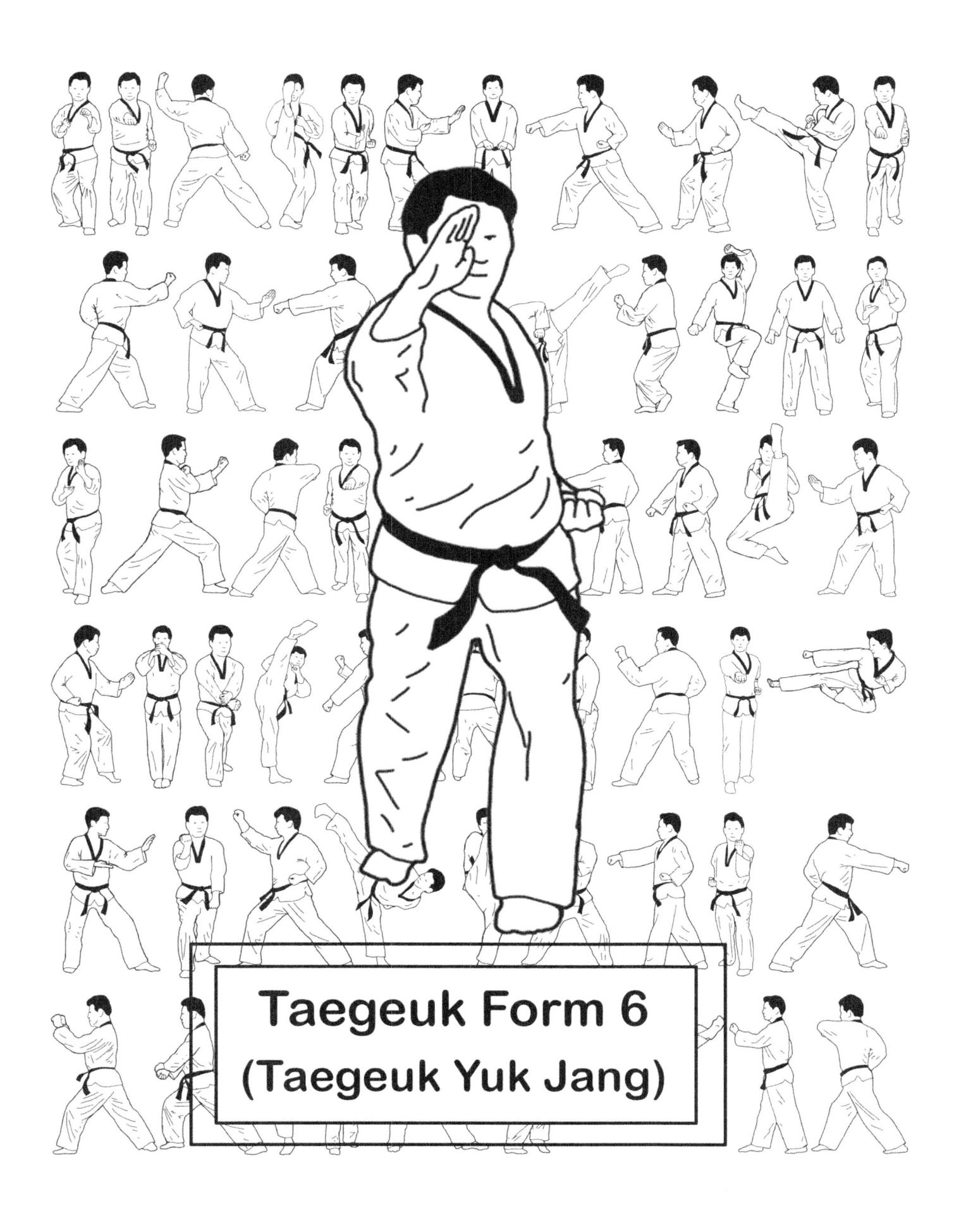

TAEGEUK YUK JANG (6)

TAEGEUK YUK JANG (6)

TAEGEUK YUK JANG (6) PART ONE

1. Ready stance
2. Front stance, low block
3. Front kick
4. Back stance, middle outward block
5. Front stance, low block
6. Front kick
7. Back stance, middle outward block
8. Front stance, reverse single knife hand high block
9. Roundhouse kick
10. Front stance, high outward block
11. Front stance, reverse middle punch
12. Front kick
13. Front stance, reverse middle punch
14. Front stance, high outward block
15. Front stance, reverse middle punch
16. Front kick
17. Front stance, reverse middle punch

TAEGEUK YUK JANG (6) PART TWO

18. Ready stance, double low block

19. Front stance, reverse single knife hand high block

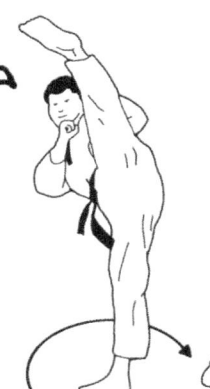

KIHAP!

20. Roundhouse kick

21. Front stance, low block

22. Front kick

23. Back stance, middle outward block

24. Front stance, low block

25. Front kick

26. Back stance, middle outward block

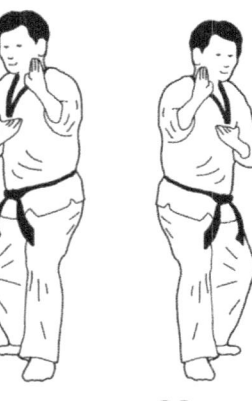

27. Back stance, knife hand middle outward block

28. Back stance, knife hand middle outward block

29. Front stance, palm hand middle block

30. Front stance, reverse middle punch

31. Front stance, palm hand middle block

32. Front stance, reverse middle punch

33. Ready stance

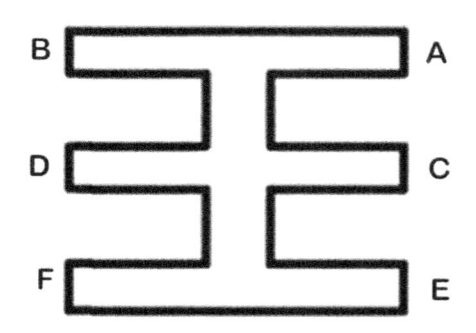

TAEGEUK YUK JANG (6)

Philosophical meaning is - Gam - symbolizing water, the ability to put yourself into a vessel, to adapt to a given situation.

This is an advanced form for blue-red belts, geup 3 and up.

This form has mostly low stances (back and front) and a kihap on a kick that is not at the end of the form.

1. Ready stance (chonbi) legs parallel, hip width (naranhi sugi).

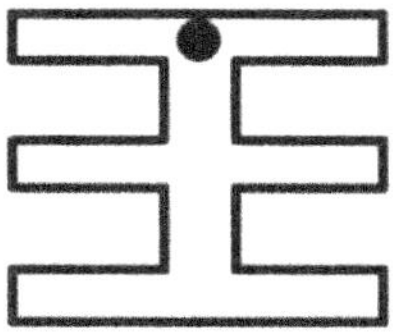

2. To your left - front stance (apkubi), low block (areh makki).

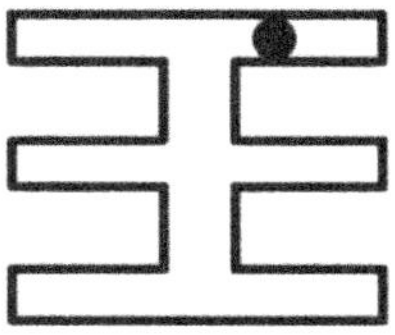

3.  Front kick (apchuck ap chagi).

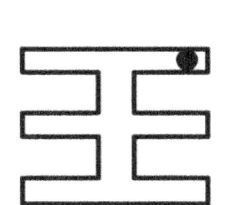

TAEGEUK YUK JANG (6)

4. Back stance (dwit kubi), middle outward block (momtong bakat makki).

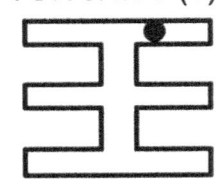

5.  (Turn via right shoulder 180 degrees). Front stance (apkubi), low block (areh makki).

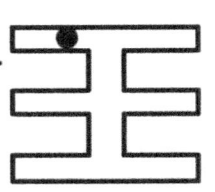

6.  Front kick (apchuck ap chagi).

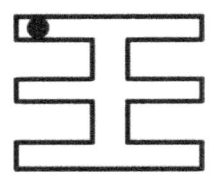

7.  Back stance (dwit kubi), middle outward block (momtong bakat makki).

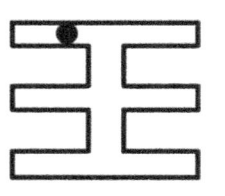

TAEGEUK YUK JANG (6)

8. Forwards –

front stance (apkubi),

half circle knife-hand high block

(hansonal ulgul bitro makki).

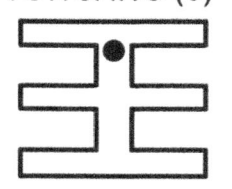

(Can be called - reverse single knife-hand high block).

9. Roundhouse kick

(dolyo chagi).

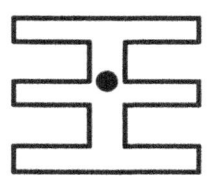

10. To your left –

front stance (apkubi),

high outward block

(ulgul bakat makki).

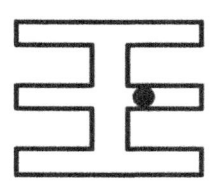

11. Front stance (apkubi),

reverse middle punch

(momtong baro jireugi).

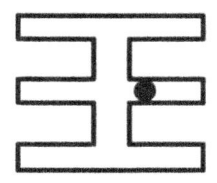

TAEGEUK YUK JANG (6)

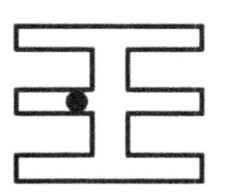

12. Front kick (apchuck ap chagi).

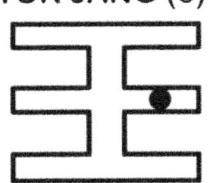

13. Front stance (apkubi), reverse middle punch (momtong baro jireugi).

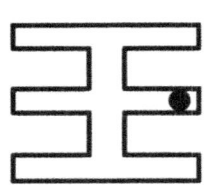

14. (Turn via right shoulder 180 degrees). Front stance (apkubi), high outward block (ulgul bakat makki).

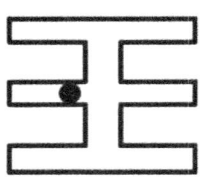

15. Front stance (apkubi), reverse middle punch (momtong baro jireugi).

TAEGEUK YUK JANG (6)

16 Front kick (apchuck ap chagi).

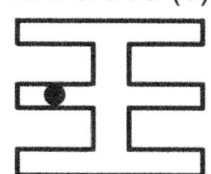

17  Front stance (apkubi), reverse middle punch (momtong baro jireugi).

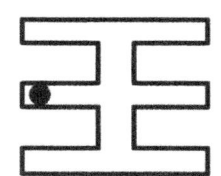

18 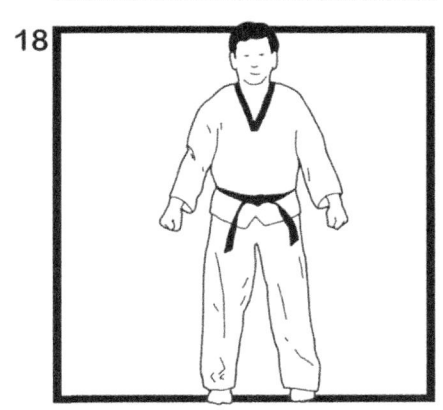 To your left – forwards - legs parallel, hip width (naranhi sugi), low section double block (areh hetcho makki).

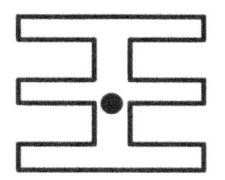

19  Front stance (apkubi), half circle knife-hand high block (hansonal ulgul bitro makki).
(Can be called - reverse single knife-hand high block).

SIDE VIEW

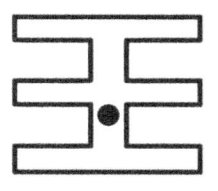

TAEGEUK YUK JANG (6)

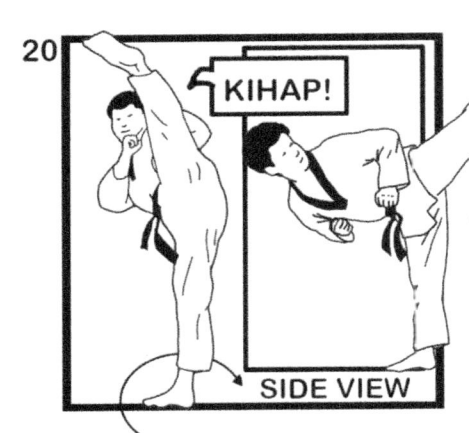

20. Roundhouse kick (dolyo chagi).
(Kick and turn 270 degrees).
Yell!

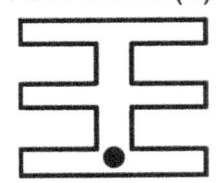

KIHAP!
SIDE VIEW

21. Front stance (apkubi), low block (areh makki).

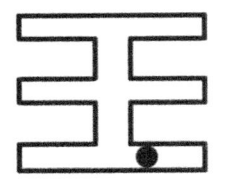

22. Front kick (apchuck ap chagi).

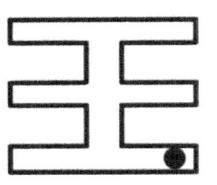

23. Back stance (dwit kubi), middle outward block (momtong bakat makki).

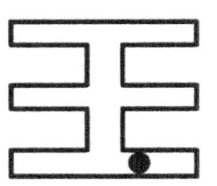

TAEGEUK YUK JANG (6)

24. (Turn via left shoulder 180 degrees) Front stance (apkubi), low block (areh makki).

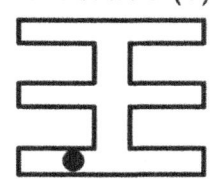

25.  Front kick (apchuck ap chagi).

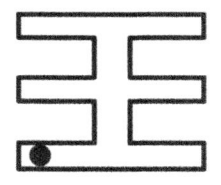

26.  Back stance (dwit kubi), middle outward block (momtong bakat makki).

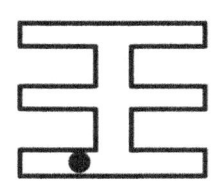

27.  Backwards facing forwards - back stance (dwit kubi), knife-hand middle block (sonal momtong makki).

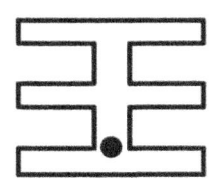

SIDE VIEW

TAEGEUK YUK JANG (6)

28. Backwards facing forwards - back stance (dwit kubi), knife-hand middle block (sonal momtong makki).

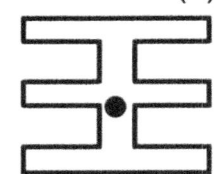

29.  Front stance (apkubi), palm hand middle block (batangson momtong makki).

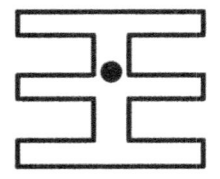

30.  Front stance (apkubi), reverse middle punch (momtong baro jireugi).

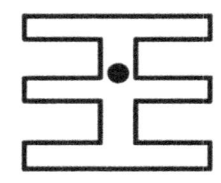

31.  Front stance (apkubi), palm hand middle block (batangson momtong makki).

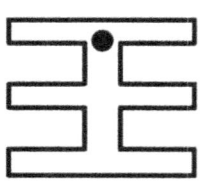

TAEGEUK YUK JANG (6)

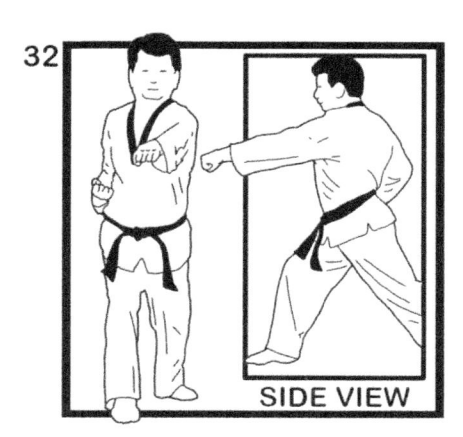

32 Front stance (apkubi), reverse middle punch (momtong baro jireugi).

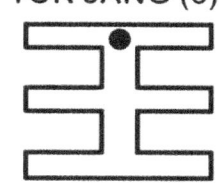

33 Move the right foot to ready stance (chonbi) legs parallel, hip width (naranhi sugi).

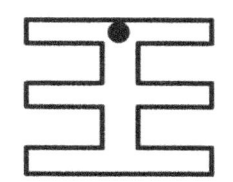

Taegeuk Form 7
(Taegeuk Chil Jang)

TAEGEUK CHIL JANG (7)

TAEGEUK CHIL JANG (7)

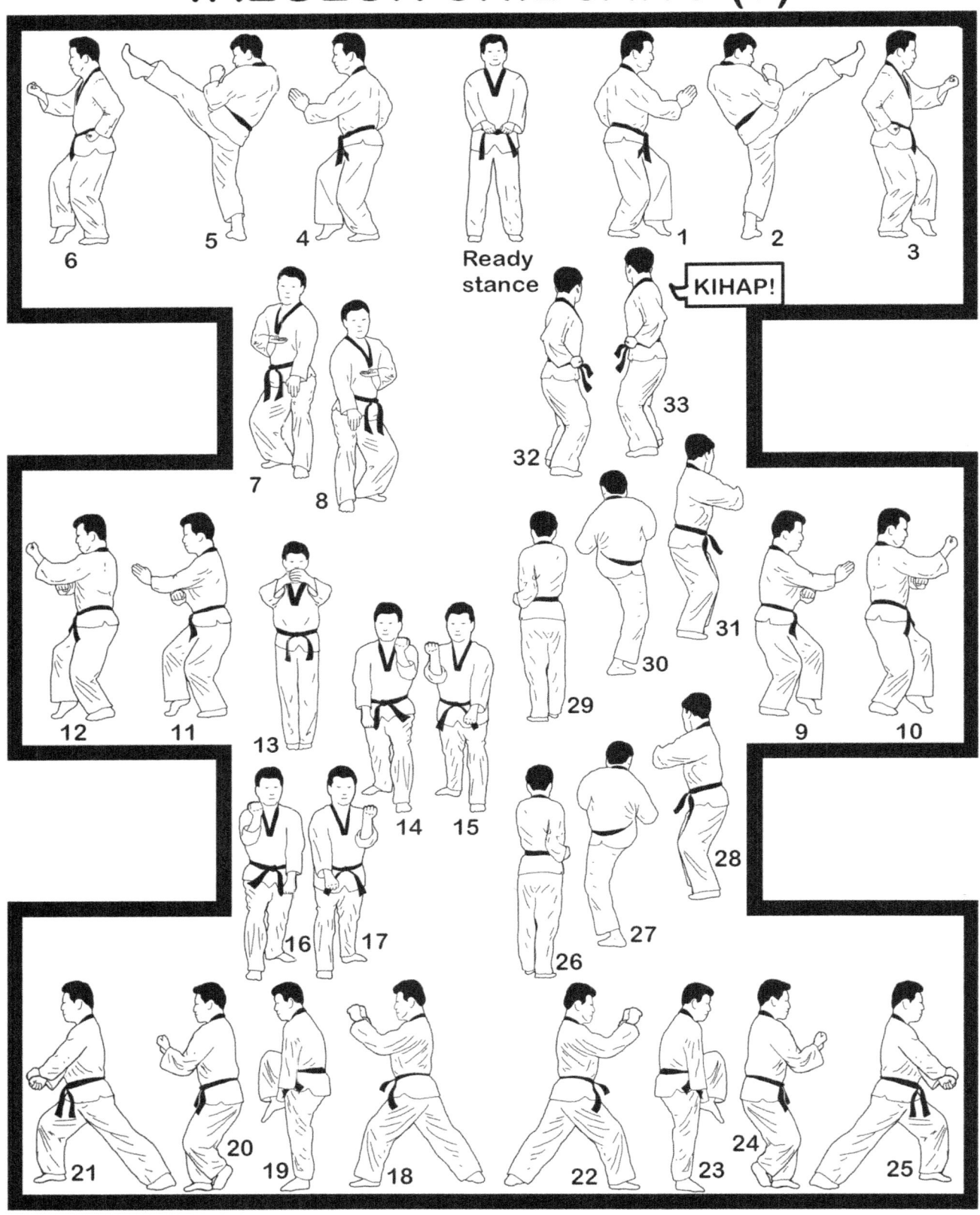

TAEGEUK CHIL JANG (7) PART ONE

1. Ready stance
2. Tiger stance, palm hand middle block 
3. Front kick 
4. Tiger stance, middle block 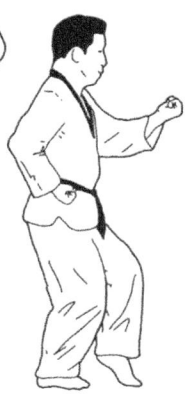
5. Tiger stance, palm hand middle block
6. Front kick 
7. Tiger stance, middle block 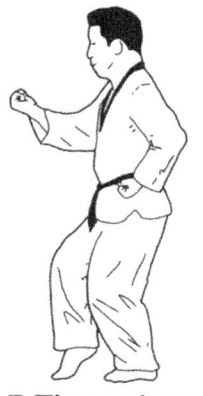
8. Back stance, knife hand low block 
9. Back stance, knife hand low block 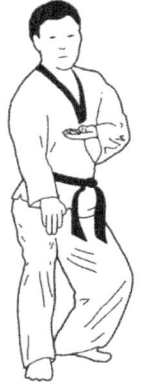
10. Tiger stance, palm hand middle block, supported 
11. Tiger stance, reverse back fist strike, supported 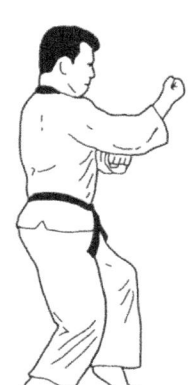
12. Tiger stance, palm hand middle block, supported 
13. Tiger stance, reverse back fist strike, supported 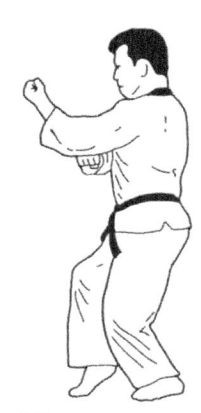
14. Closed stance, covered fist 
15. Front stance, reverse scissors block 
16. Front stance, scissors block 
17. Front stance, reverse scissors block 
18. Front stance, scissors block 
19. Front stance, outer middle wedge block 
20. Knee kick

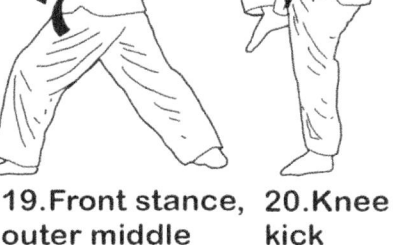

TAEGEUK CHIL JANG (7) PART TWO

21. Cross stance, double middle uppercut punch

22. Front stance, low x – block

23. Front stance, outer middle wedge block

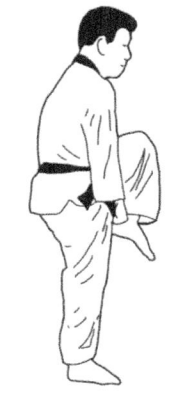

24. Knee kick

25. Cross stance, double middle uppercut punch

26. Front stance, low x – block

27. Walking stance, back fist outward strike

28. Crescent kick to palm

29. Horse stance, elbow strike to palm

30. Walking stance, back fist outward strike

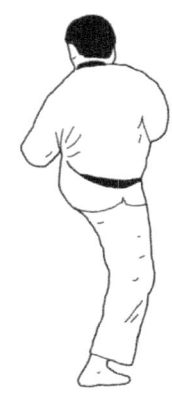

31. Crescent kick to palm

32. Horse stance, elbow strike to palm

33. Horse stance, sideways single knife hand

34. Horse stance, middle side punch

KIHAP!

35. Ready stance

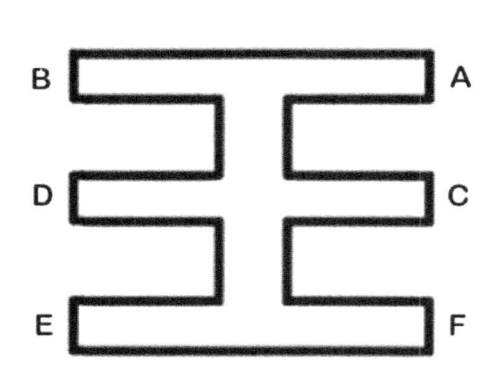

TAEGEUK CHIL JANG (7)

Philosophical meaning - Gan - which symbolizes a mountain, very stable. The method of Taekwondo means that stability is a very important element which keeps the continuum, the ability to do attack / defense techniques. We can see how the stability is present in the poomsae – be it in the stances (tiger stance, which is hard to be stable in, and the horse stance which is very stable – and also looks like a mountain) and also the covered fist – which comes from below like a mountain, rising upwards.

Suitable for the red-brown belts, geup 2 and up.

1. Ready stance (chonbi) legs parallel, hip width (naranhi sugi).

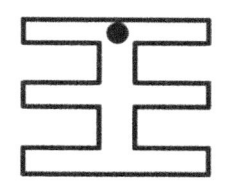

2.  To your left - tiger stance (beom sugi), palm hand middle block (batangson momtong makki).

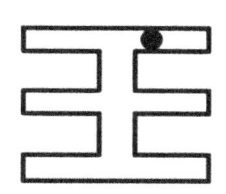

3.  Front kick (apchuck ap chagi).

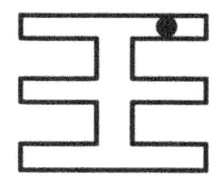

101

TAEGEUK CHIL JANG (7)

4. Tiger stance (beom sugi), middle block (momtong makki).

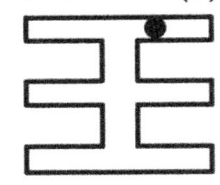

5.  (Turn via right shoulder 180 degrees). Tiger stance (beom sugi), palm hand middle block (batangson momtong makki).

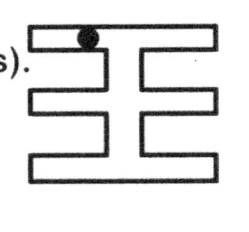

6.  Front kick (apchuck ap chagi).

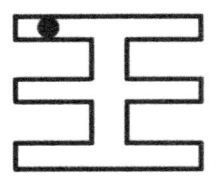

7. 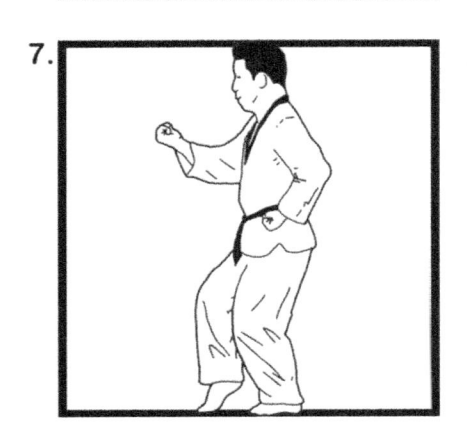 Tiger stance (beom sugi), middle block (momtong makki).

102

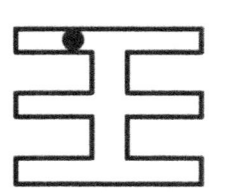

TAEGEUK CHIL JANG (7)

8. Forwards -
back stance (dwit kubi),
knife-hand low block
(sonal areh makki).

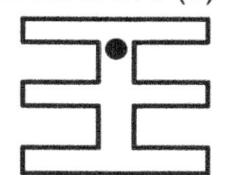

9. Back stance (dwit kubi),
knife-hand low block
(sonal areh makki).

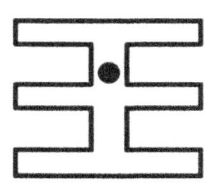

10. To your left -
tiger stance (beom sugi),
palm hand middle block supported
(batangson momtong godureo an makki).

11. Tiger stance (beom sugi),
reverse back fist strike,
supported (dong jumeok apchigi).

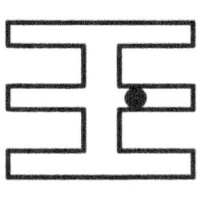

TAEGEUK CHIL JANG (7)

12 (Turn via right shoulder 180 degrees).

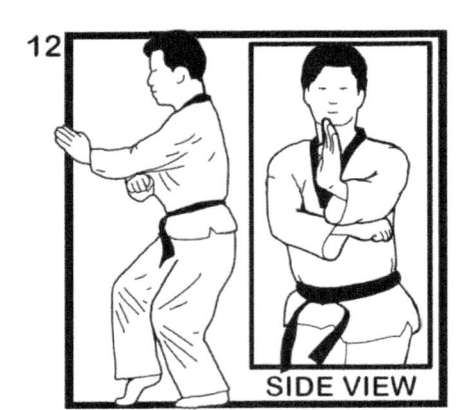

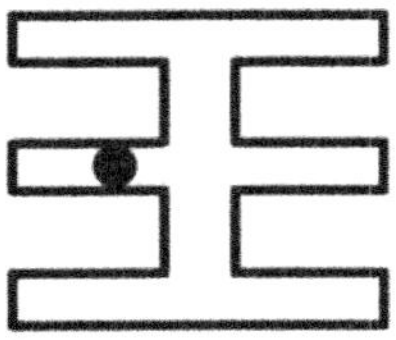

Tiger stance (beom sugi),

palm hand middle block supported

(batangson momtong godureo an makki).

13 Tiger stance (beom sugi),

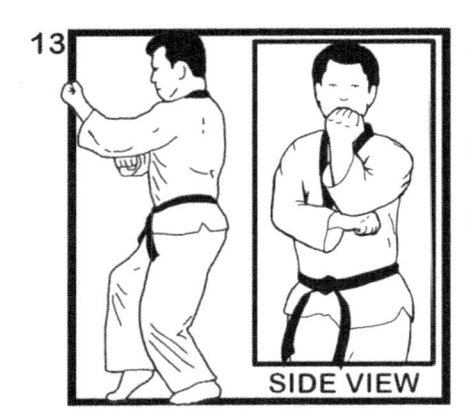

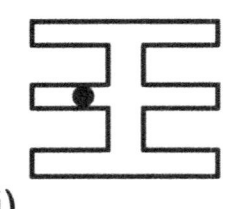

reverse back fist strike,

supported (dong jumeok apchigi).

14 Forward -

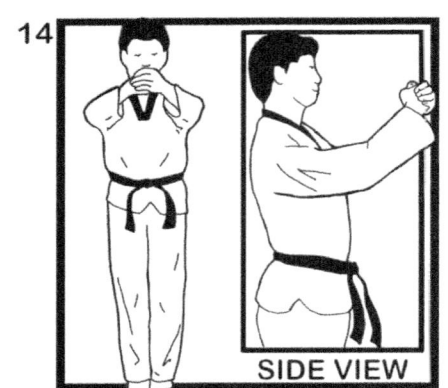

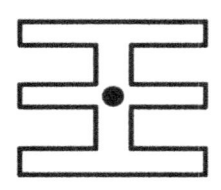

closed stance (moa sugi),

covering fist (bo jumeok).

15 Front stance (apkubi),

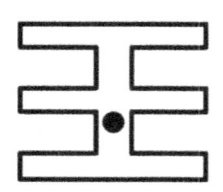

scissors block (gawi makki),

TAEGEUK CHIL JANG (7)

16. Front stance (apkubi), scissors block (gawi makki).

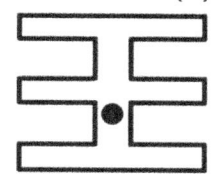

17.  Front stance (apkubi), scissors block (gawi makki).

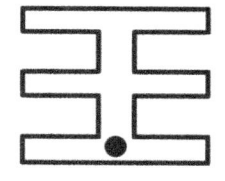

18.  Front stance (apkubi), scissors block (gawi makki).

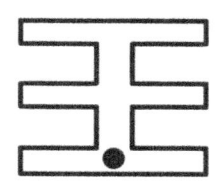

19.  (Turn 270 degrees via left shoulder).

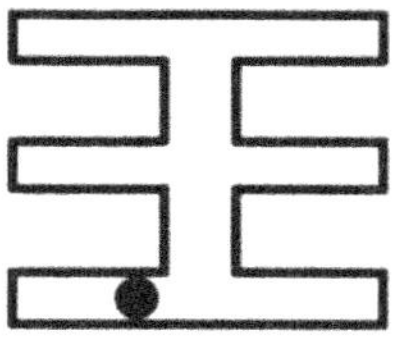

Front stance (apkubi), outer wrist middle wedge block / double block (hecho momtong makki).

TAEGEUK CHIL JANG (7)

20. Knee strike (morop chagi).

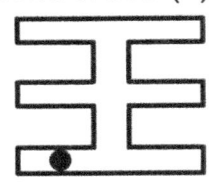

21.  Cross stance (kua sugi), double uppercut middle section punch (dujumeok jeochojireugi).

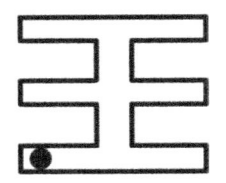

22. 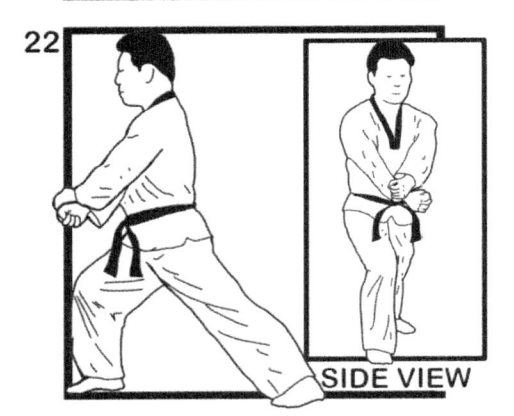 Front stance (apkubi), low section x - block (otkoreo areh makki).

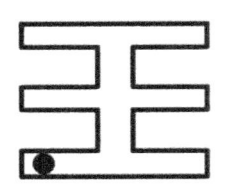

23.  (Turn 180 degrees via right shoulder).
Front stance (apkubi), outer wrist middle wedge block / double block (hecho momtong makki).

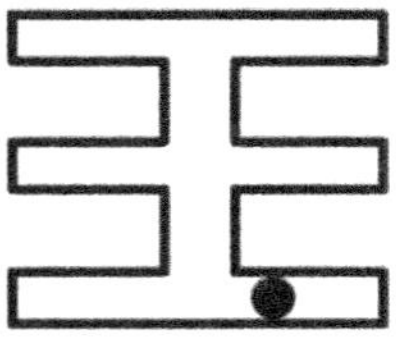

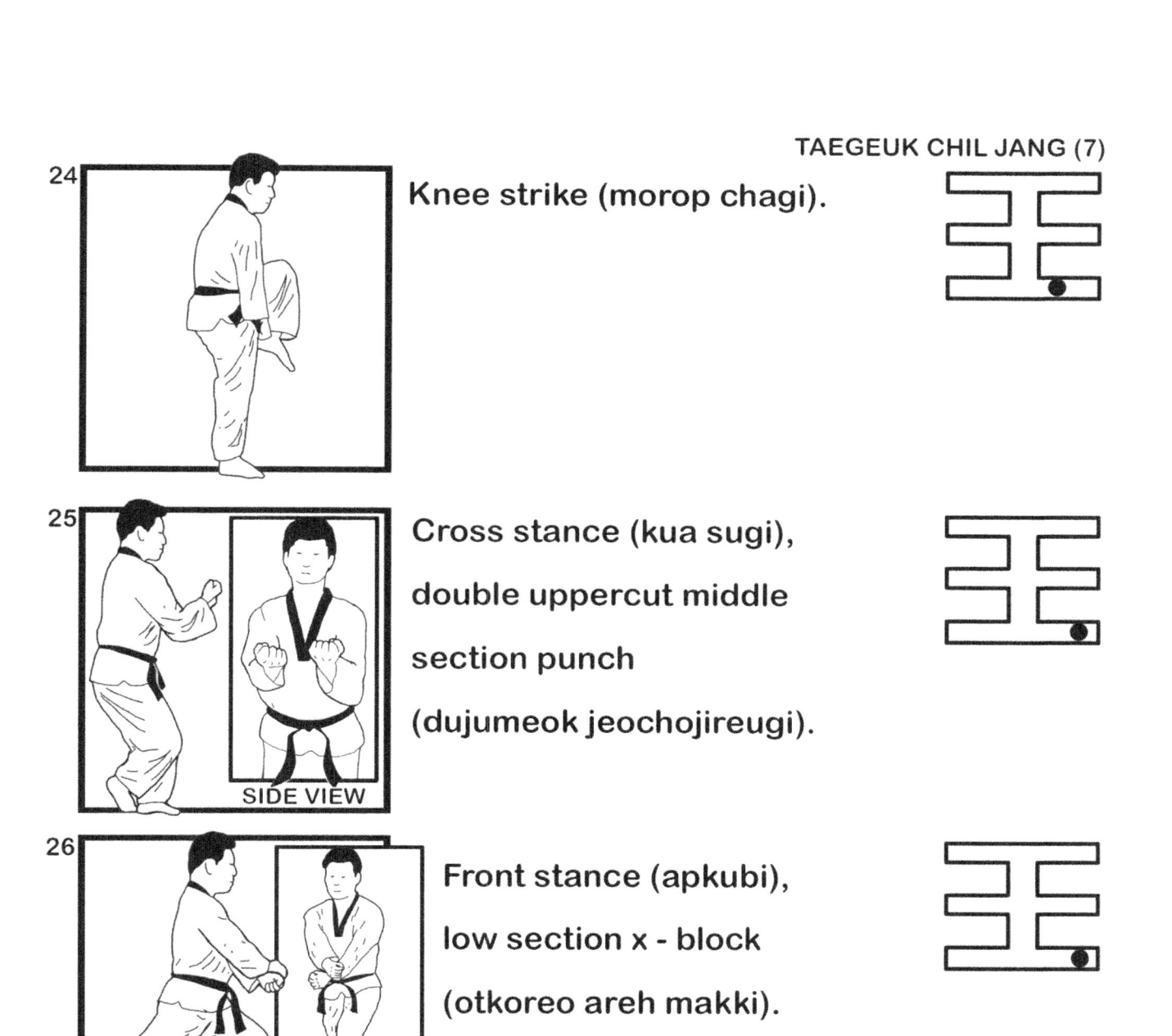

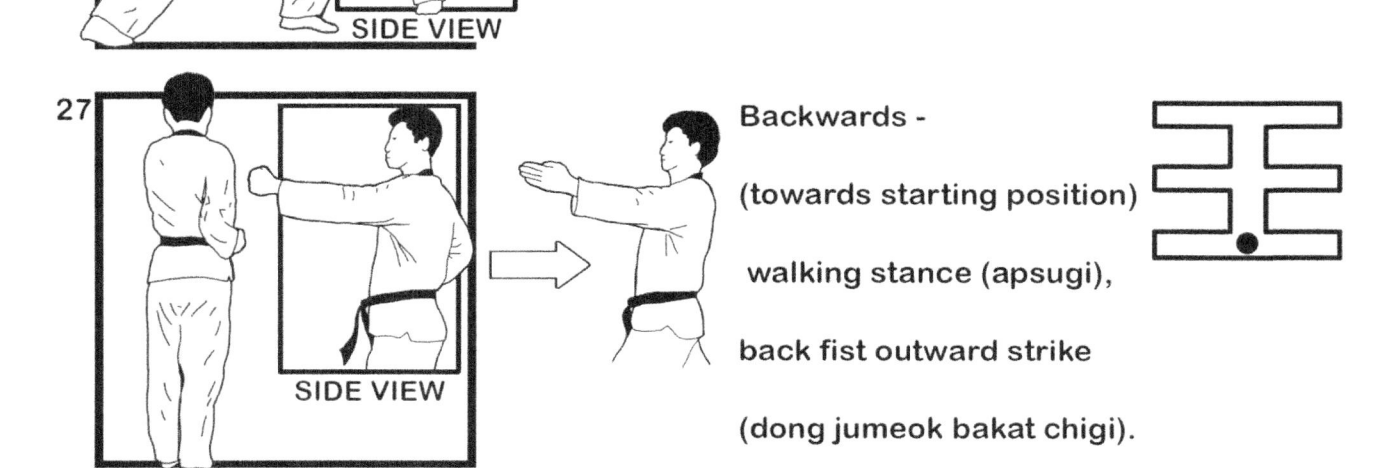

TAEGEUK CHIL JANG (7)

24. Knee strike (morop chagi).

25. Cross stance (kua sugi), double uppercut middle section punch (dujumeok jeochojireugi).

26. Front stance (apkubi), low section x - block (otkoreo areh makki).

27. Backwards - (towards starting position) walking stance (apsugi), back fist outward strike (dong jumeok bakat chigi).

TAEGEUK CHIL JANG (7)

28. Inner crescent kick to the palm (pyojeok chagi).

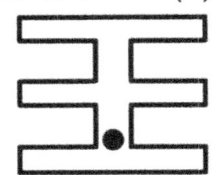

29. 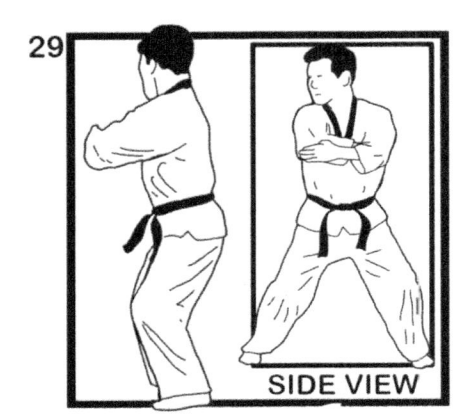 Horse-riding stance (juchum sugi), elbow target strike (palkup pyojeok chigi).

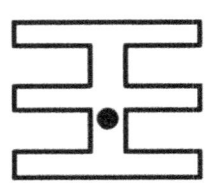

30. 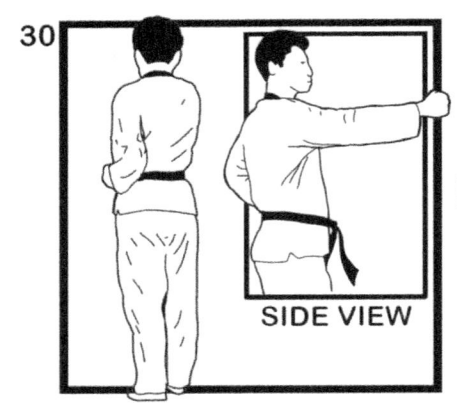 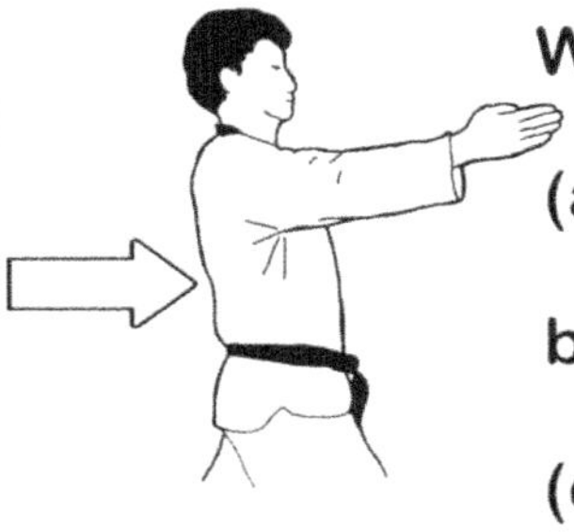 Walking stance (apsugi), back fist outward strike (dong jumeok bakat chigi).

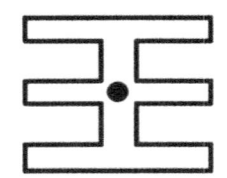

31. 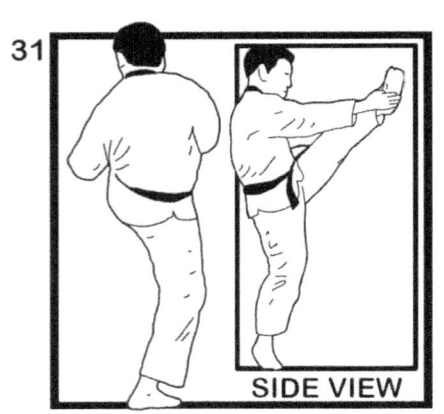 Inner crescent kick to the palm (pyojeok chagi).

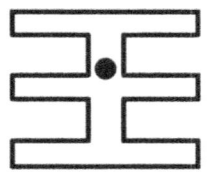

TAEGEUK CHIL JANG (7)

32 Horse-riding stance (juchum sugi), elbow target strike (palkup pyojeok chigi).

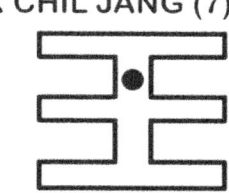

33 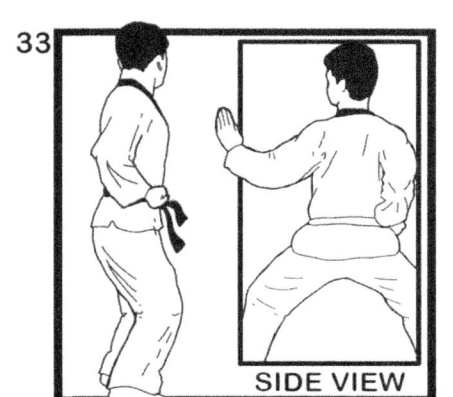 Horse-riding stance (juchum sugi), single knife-hand middle side block (hansonal momtong yop makki).

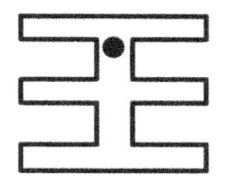

34  Horse-riding stance (juchum sugi), middle side punch (momtong yop jireugi). Yell!

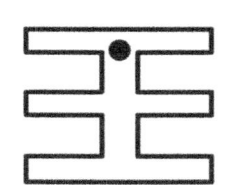

35  (Move the left leg back to the starting position). Ready stance (chonbi) legs parallel, hip width (naranhi sugi).

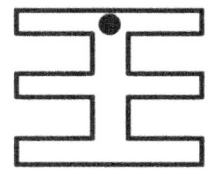

Taegeuk Form 8
(Taegeuk Pal Jang)

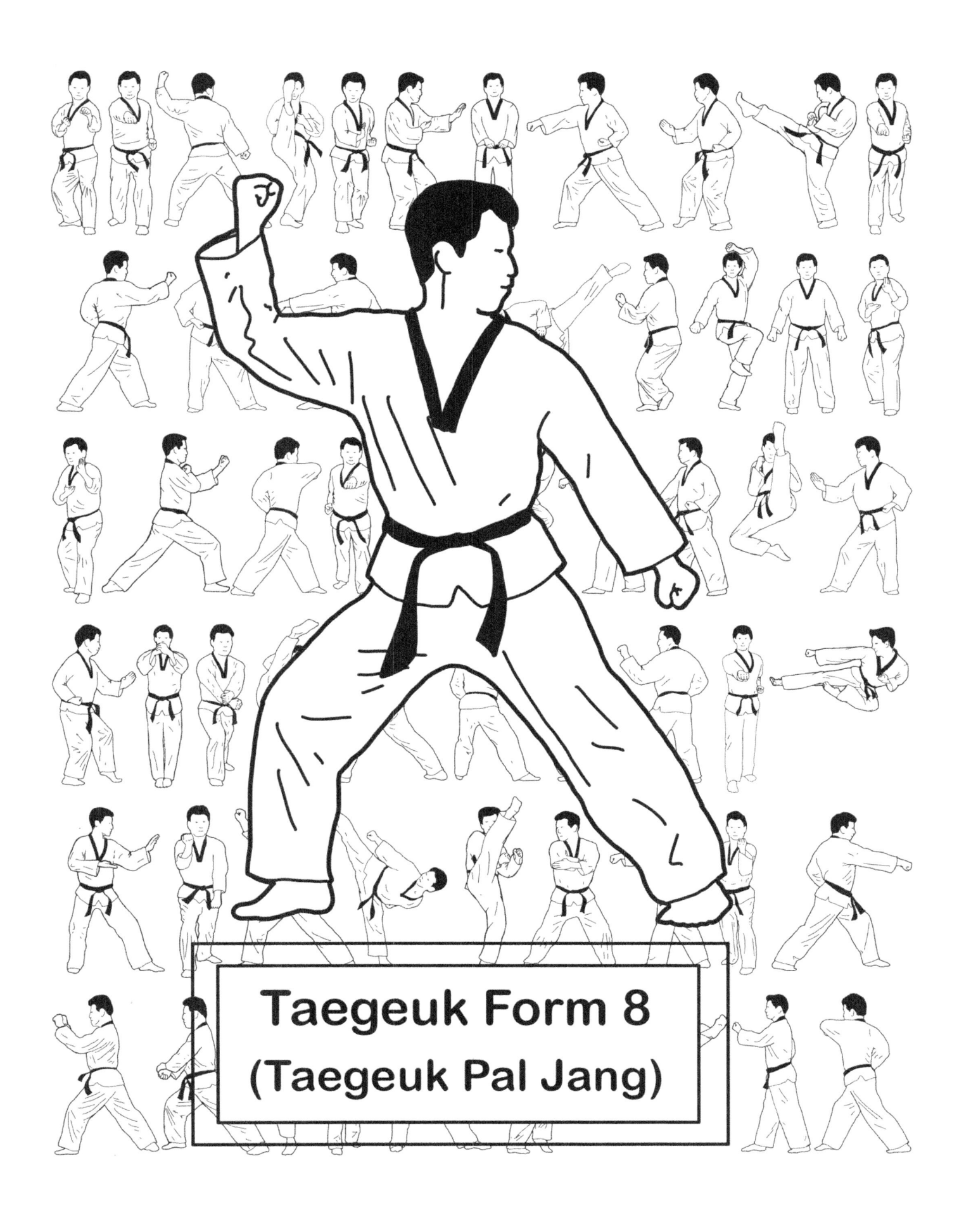

TAEGEUK PAL JANG (8)

TAEGEUK PAL JANG (8)

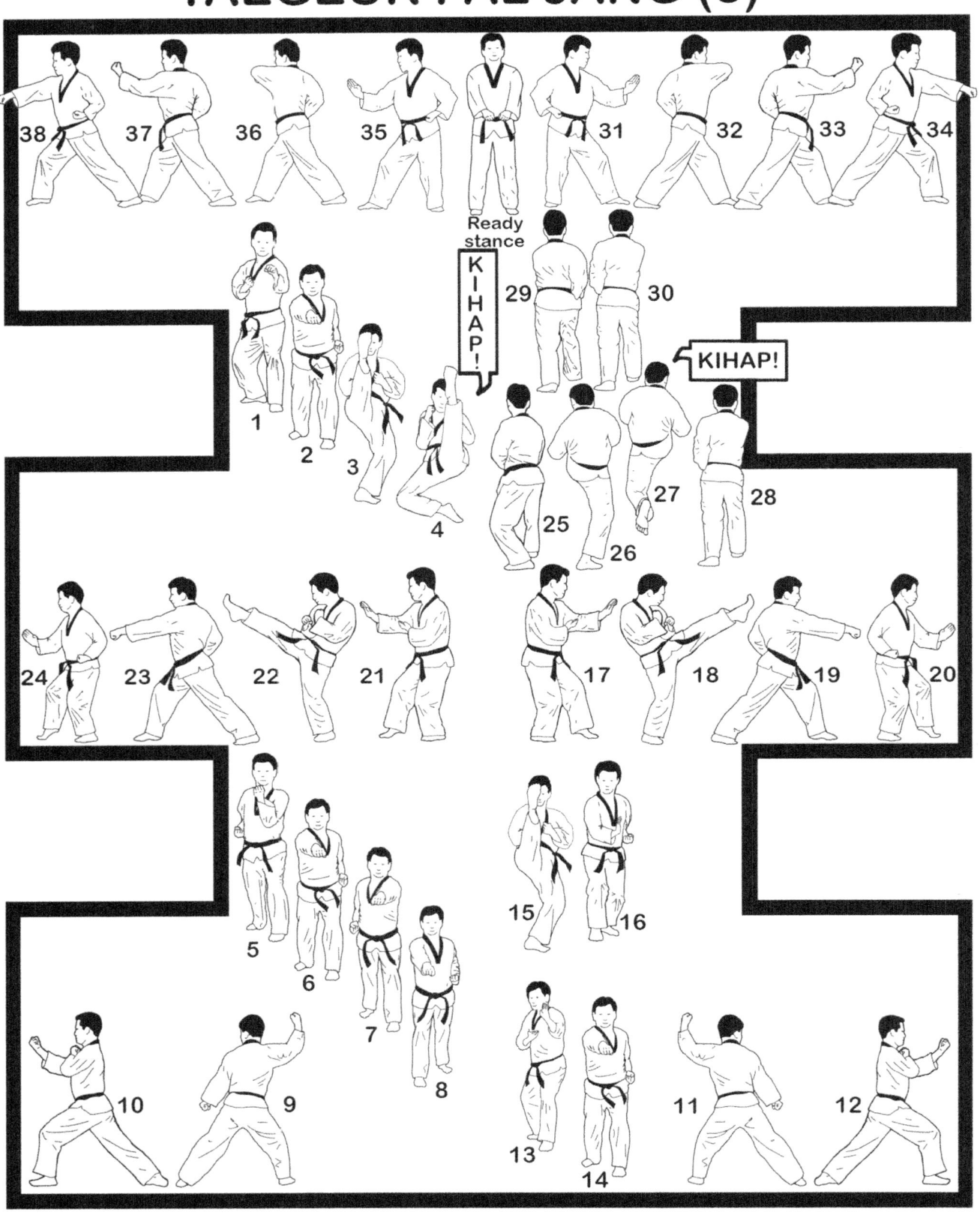

TAEGEUK PAL JANG (8) PART ONE

KIHAP!

1. Ready stance
2. Back stance, supporting middle block 
3. Front stance, reverse middle punch 
4. Front kick
5. Hopping front kick
6. Front stance, middle block 
7. Front stance, reverse middle punch 
8. Front stance, middle punch 
9. Front stance, middle punch 
10. Front stance, single mountain block 
11. Front stance, pulling uppercut 
12. Front stance, single mountain block 
13. Front stance, pulling uppercut 
14. Back stance, middle knife hand block 
15. Front stance, reverse middle punch 
16. Front kick 

115

TAEGEUK PAL JANG (8) PART TWO

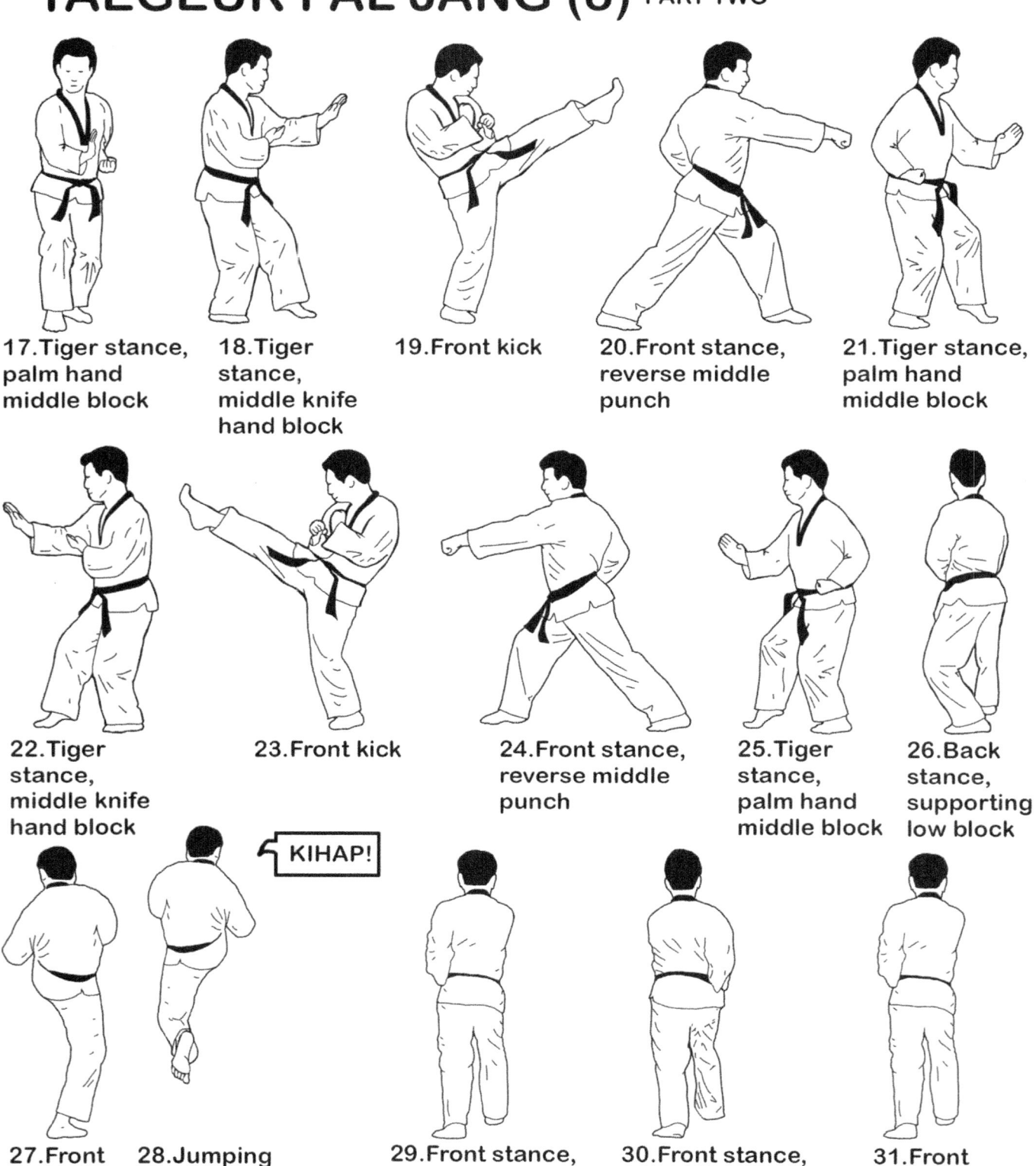

17. Tiger stance, palm hand middle block

18. Tiger stance, middle knife hand block

19. Front kick

20. Front stance, reverse middle punch

21. Tiger stance, palm hand middle block

22. Tiger stance, middle knife hand block

23. Front kick

24. Front stance, reverse middle punch

25. Tiger stance, palm hand middle block

26. Back stance, supporting low block

27. Front kick

28. Jumping front kick

KIHAP!

29. Front stance, middle block

30. Front stance, reverse middle punch

31. Front stance, middle punch

TAEGEUK PAL JANG (8) PART THREE

32. Back stance, single knife hand middle block

33. Front stance, reverse elbow strike

34. Front stance, reverse back fist front strike

35. Front stance, middle punch

36. Back stance, single knife hand middle block

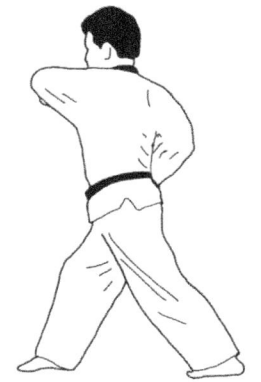

37. Front stance, reverse elbow strike

38. Front stance, reverse back fist front strike

39. Front stance, middle punch

40. Ready stance

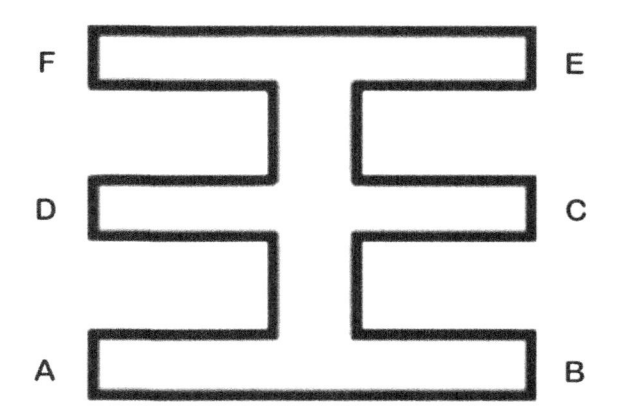

TAEGEUK PAL JANG (8)

Philosophical meaning – Gon – which symbolizes Earth, pure Yin.

This is the closing of the circle and the final principal of the 8 elements in the different trigrams. The Yin is the principal of acceptance, being receptive.

This is the last poomsae to be studied and known before the black belt. It is for geup 1 and up (after geup 1 you move to the rank of Dan 1 – black belt). This poomsae contains many complicated techniques and two kihaps done during the jumping kicks.

1. Ready stance (chonbi) legs parallel, hip width (naranhi sugi).

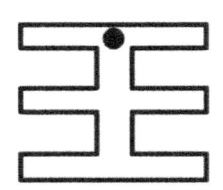

2. Forward - back stance (dwit kubi), supporting middle block (momtong godureo bakkat makki).

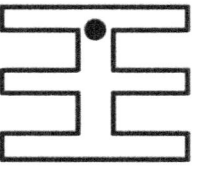

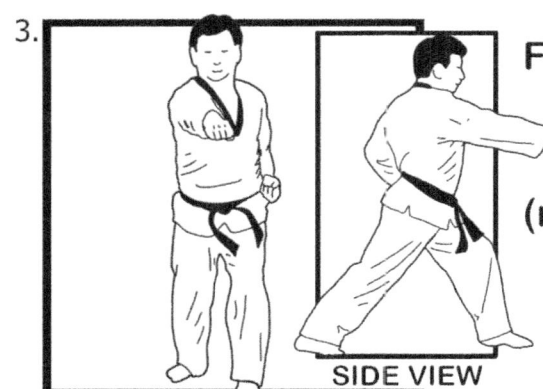

3. Front stance (apkubi), reverse middle punch (momtong baro jireugi).

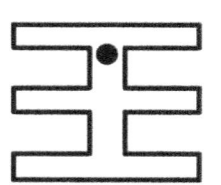

SIDE VIEW

TAEGEUK PAL JANG (8)

4. Front kick (apchuck ap chagi).

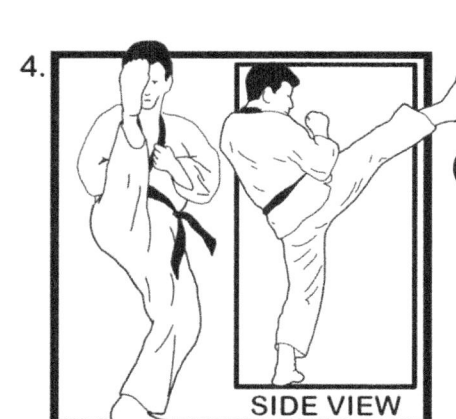

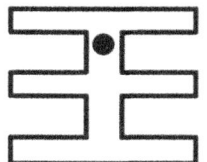

SIDE VIEW

5.  Hopping front kick (dupal dangsang ap chagi). Yell!

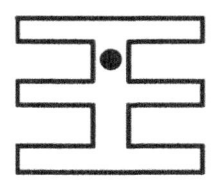

KIHAP!

6. 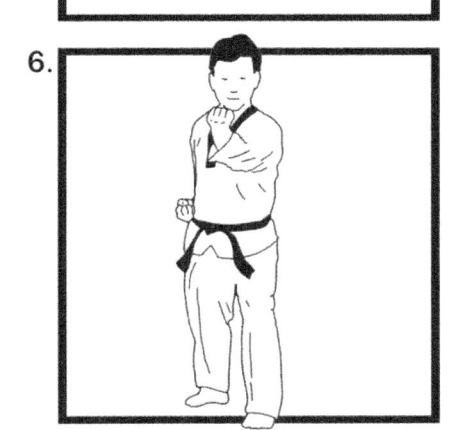 Front stance (apkubi), middle block from outside in (momtong makki).

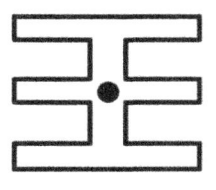

7. 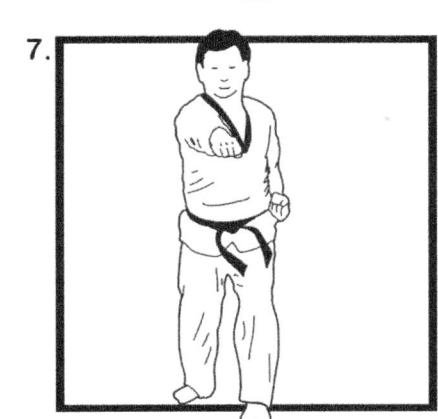 Front stance (apkubi), reverse middle punch (momtong baro jireugi).

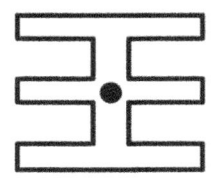

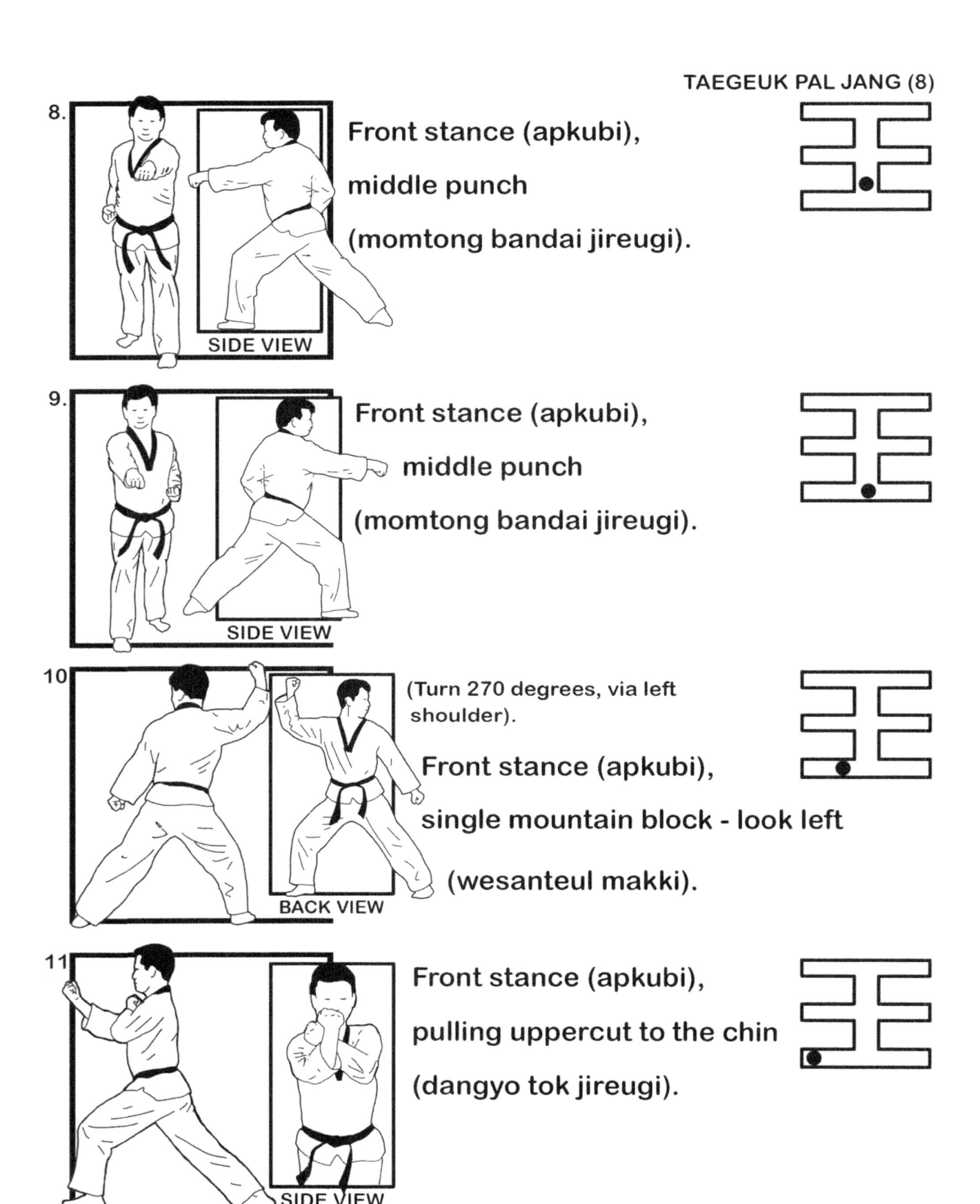

TAEGEUK PAL JANG (8)

8. Front stance (apkubi), middle punch (momtong bandai jireugi).

9. Front stance (apkubi), middle punch (momtong bandai jireugi).

10. (Turn 270 degrees, via left shoulder).
Front stance (apkubi), single mountain block - look left (wesanteul makki).

11. Front stance (apkubi), pulling uppercut to the chin (dangyo tok jireugi).

120

TAEGEUK PAL JANG (8)

12 (Remain on the same line, do a cross stance to your right).

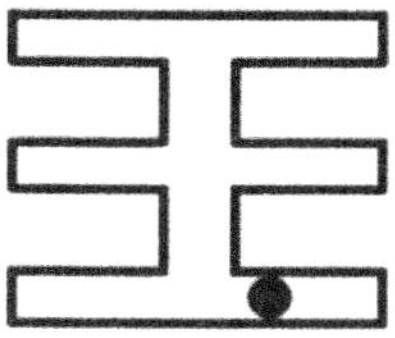

Front stance (apkubi), single mountain block - look right (wesanteul makki).

13 Front stance (apkubi), pulling uppercut to the chin (dangyo tok jireugi).

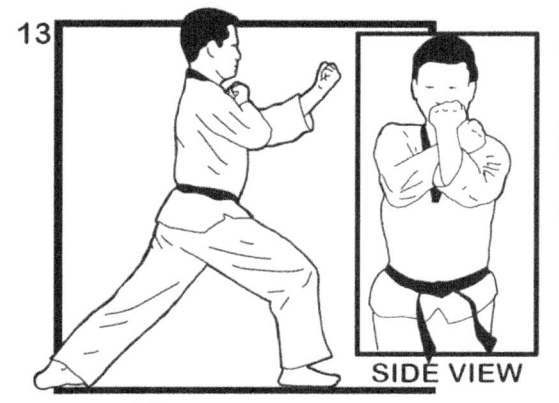

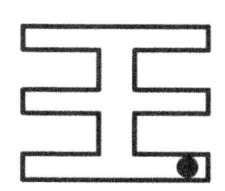

14  (Backwards, 270 degrees, via left shoulder).

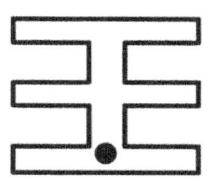

Back stance (dwit kubi), knife-hand middle outward block (sonal momtong makki).

15 Front stance (apkubi), reverse middle punch (momtong baro jireugi).

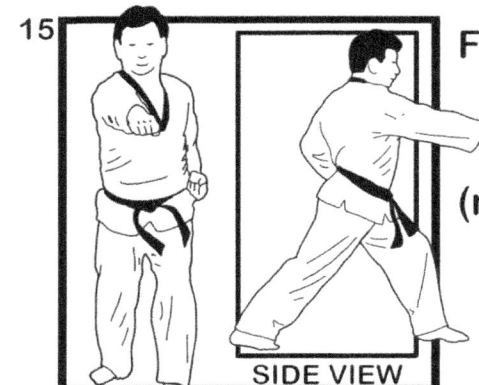

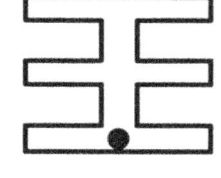

TAEGEUK PAL JANG (8)

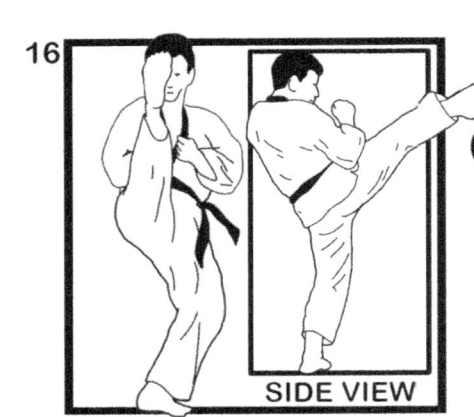

16. Front kick (apchuck ap chagi).

SIDE VIEW

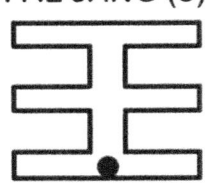

17. {Bring the kicking leg back (right leg), take another step back, and then a small step to tiger stance},

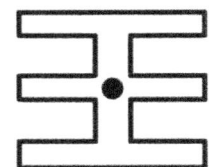

Tiger stance (beom sugi), palm hand middle block (batangson momtong makki).

SIDE VIEW

18. Turn to left - tiger stance (beom sugi), knife-hand middle outward block (sonal momtong makki).

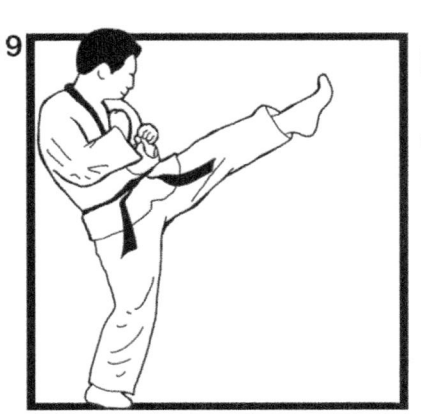

BACK VIEW

19. Front kick (apchuck ap chagi), with the front leg.

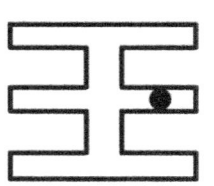

TAEGEUK PAL JANG (8)

20. Front stance (apkubi), reverse middle punch (momtong baro jireugi).

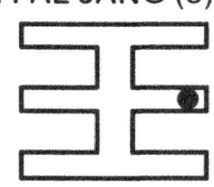

21.  (Bring the left leg back). Tiger stance (beom sugi), palm hand middle block (batangson momtong makki).

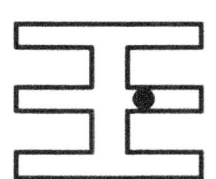

22.  (Turn via right shoulder 180 degrees). Tiger stance (beom sugi), knife-hand middle outward block (sonal momtong makki).

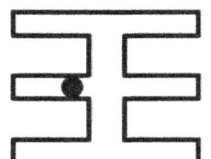

BACK VIEW

23.  Front kick (apchuck ap chagi), with the front leg.

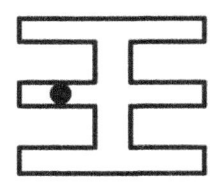

123

TAEGEUK PAL JANG (8)

24. Front stance (apkubi), reverse middle punch (momtong baro jireugi).

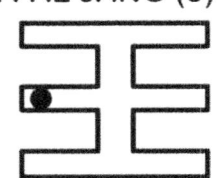

25. (Bring the right leg back).
Tiger stance (beom sugi), palm hand middle block (batangson momtong makki).

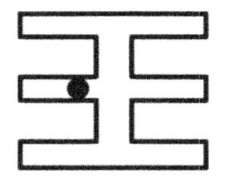

26. Backwards -
back stance (dwit kubi), supporting low section block (godureo areh makki).

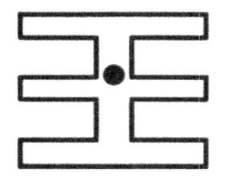

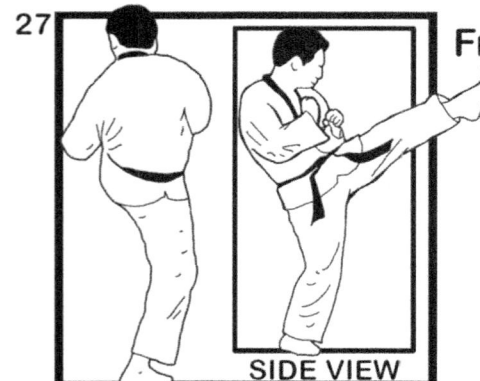

SIDE VIEW

27. Front kick (apchuck ap chagi).

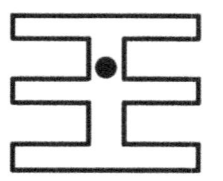

SIDE VIEW

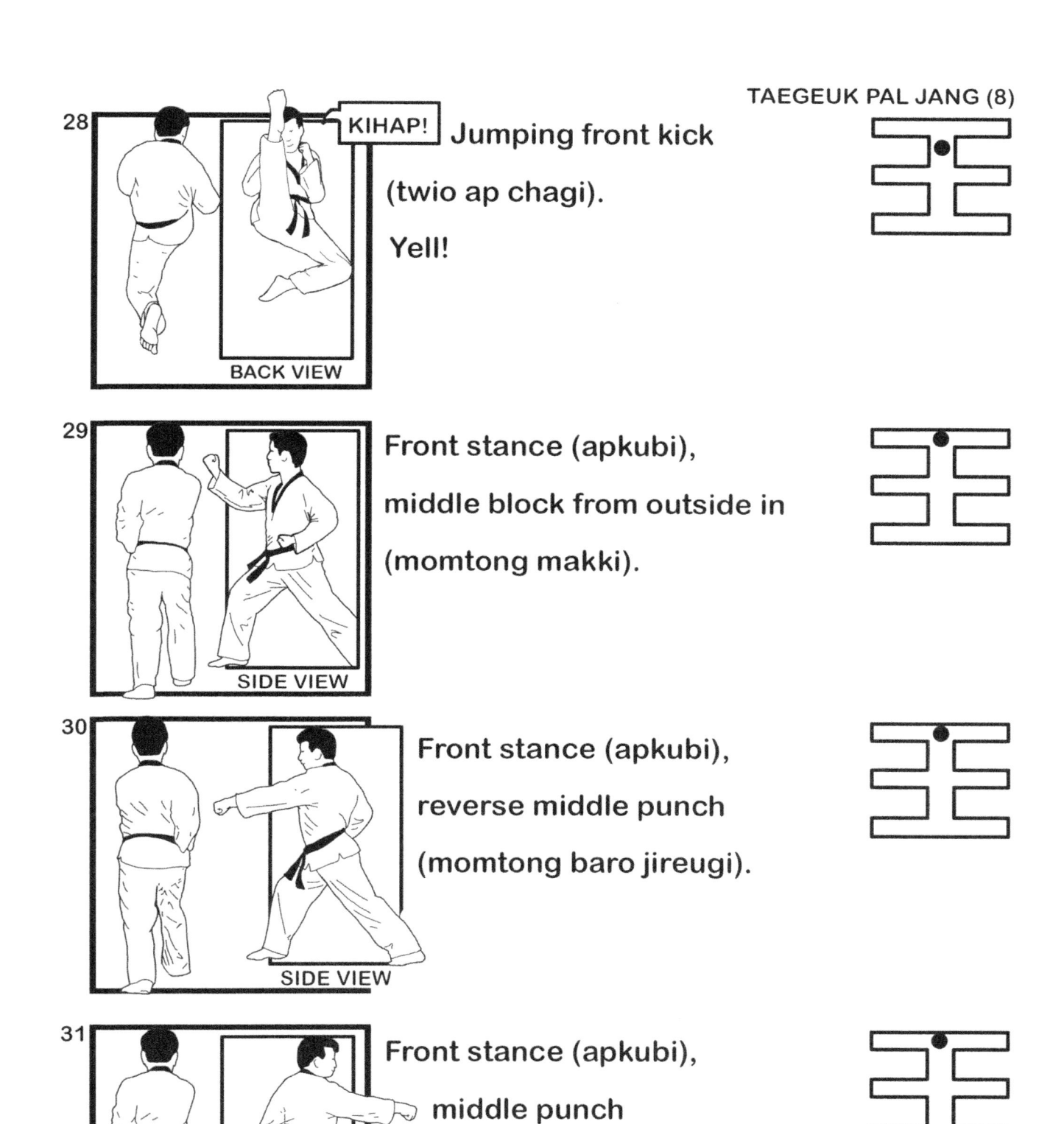

TAEGEUK PAL JANG (8)

28. Jumping front kick (twio ap chagi). Yell! KIHAP! BACK VIEW

29. Front stance (apkubi), middle block from outside in (momtong makki). SIDE VIEW

30. Front stance (apkubi), reverse middle punch (momtong baro jireugi). SIDE VIEW

31. Front stance (apkubi), middle punch (momtong bandai jireugi). SIDE VIEW

TAEGEUK PAL JANG (8)

32 (Turn via left shoulder 270 degrees).

Back stance (dwit kubi), single knife-hand middle outward block (hansonal momtong makki).

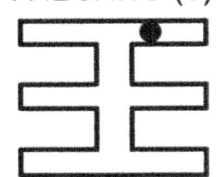

33  Front stance (apkubi), elbow round strike (palkup dollyochigi).

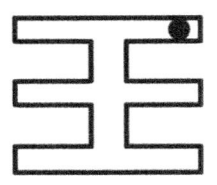

34  Front stance (apkubi), back fist front strike (dong jumeok apachigi).

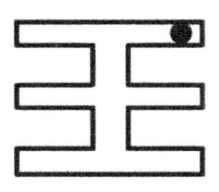

35  Front stance (apkubi), middle punch (momtong bandai jireugi).

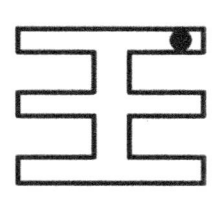

TAEGEUK PAL JANG (8)

36. (Turn via right shoulder 180 degrees). Back stance (dwit kubi), single knife-hand middle outward block (hansonal momtong makki).

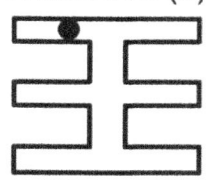

37.  Front stance (apkubi), elbow round strike (palkup dollyochigi).

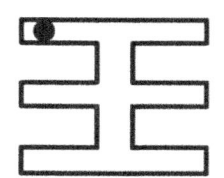

BACK VIEW

38.  Front stance (apkubi), back fist front strike (dong jumeok apachigi).

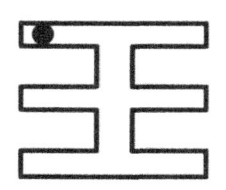

39.  Front stance (apkubi), middle punch (momtong bandai jireugi).

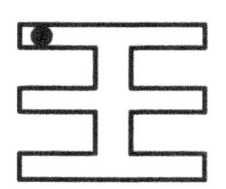

127

TAEGEUK PAL JANG (8)

40

(Move the right leg back to the starting position).

Ready stance (chonbi) legs parallel, hip width (naranhi sugi).

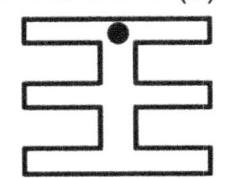

Second part – techniques and more:

Basic and advanced techniques

Basic explanations for executing Taekwondo techniques:

- Most of the kicks start with a bent leg.
- When you do a block, pay attention that the elbow does not go out of the body-line.
- When you prepare to perform a technique, inhale.
- When you perform it, exhale.
- When you do a stance, pay attention that your back is straight and perpendicular to the floor.
- When you do a technique, block/kick/attack, you have to know which part of the body will hit the target (ball of the foot, heel, knuckles, etc).
- When you attack – focus and aim to hit the precise target.
- The part that generates the power in Taekwondo is the hip! Pay attention to always move the hip while doing blocks and attacks!

In the following pages, you will find several Taekwondo techniques both basic and advanced.

BASIC STANCES

Back stance (dwit kubi)

Horse-riding stance (juchum sugi)

Closed stance (moa sugi)

Ready stance (chonbi) legs parallel, hip width (naranhi sugi)

Front stance (apkubi)

Walking stance (apsugi)

ADVANCED STANCES

Tiger stance (beom sugi)

Cross stance (kua sugi)

Crane stance (hakdari sugi)

BASIC BLOCKS

High block (ulgul makki)

Reverse middle block from outside in (momtong an makki)

Middle outward block (bakat palmok momtong bakat makki)

Middle outward block (an palmok momtong bakat makki)

Low block (areh makki)

High outward block (ulgul bakat makki)

ADVANCED BLOCKS

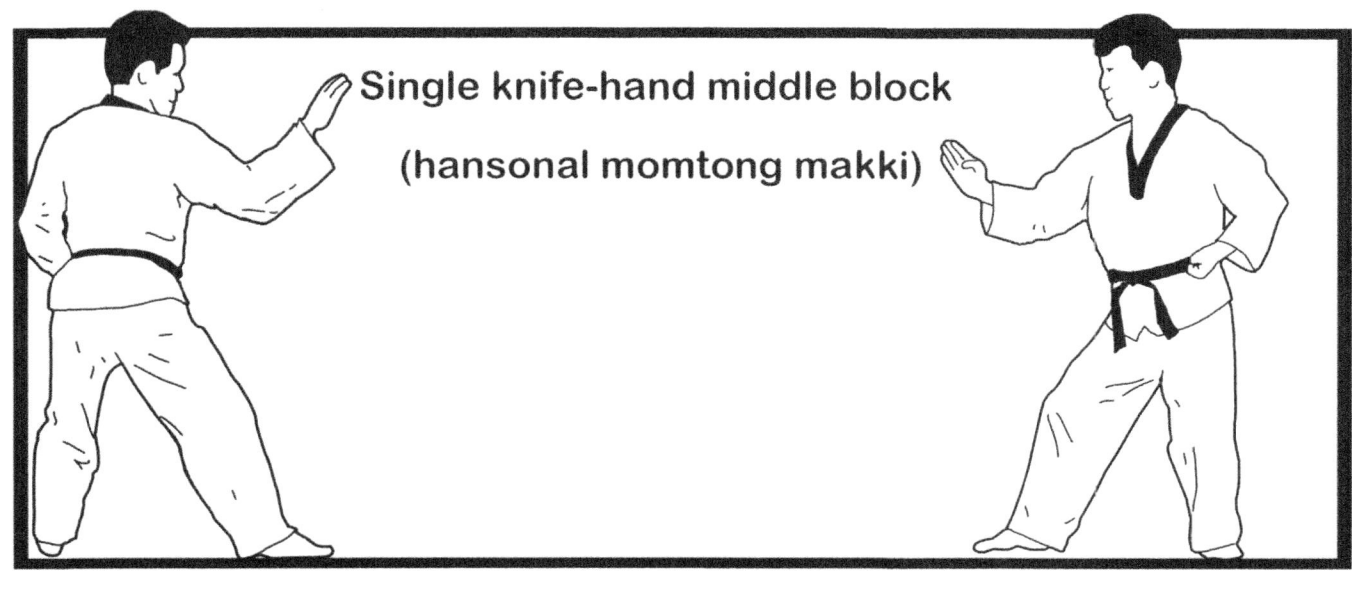

Low section double block (areh hetcho makki)

Knife-hand low block (sonal areh makki)

Outer wrist middle wedge block/ double block (hecho momtong makki)

Supporting middle block (momtong godureo bakkat makki)

Single knife-hand middle block (hansonal momtong makki)

ADVANCED BLOCKS

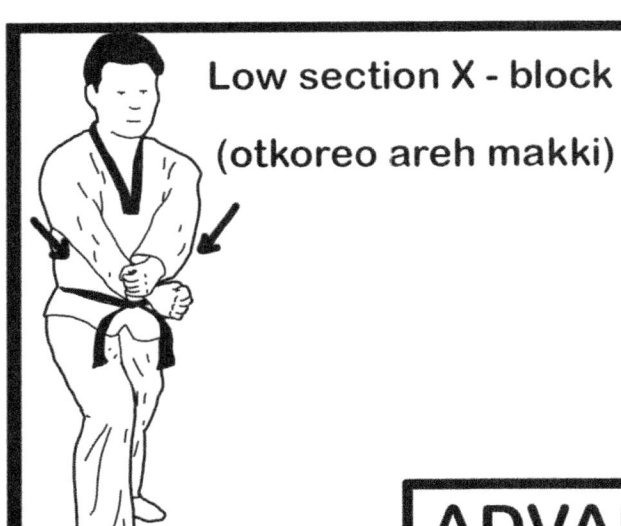

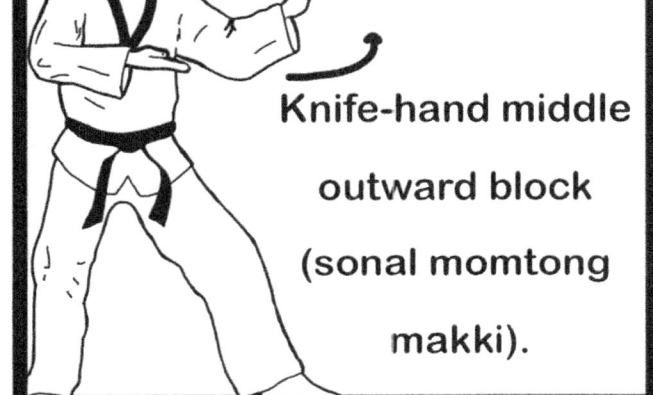

Low section X - block (otkoreo areh makki)

Palm hand middle block (batangson momtong makki)

Knife-hand middle outward block (sonal momtong makki).

Single mountain block (wesanteul makki)

Scissors block (gawi makki)

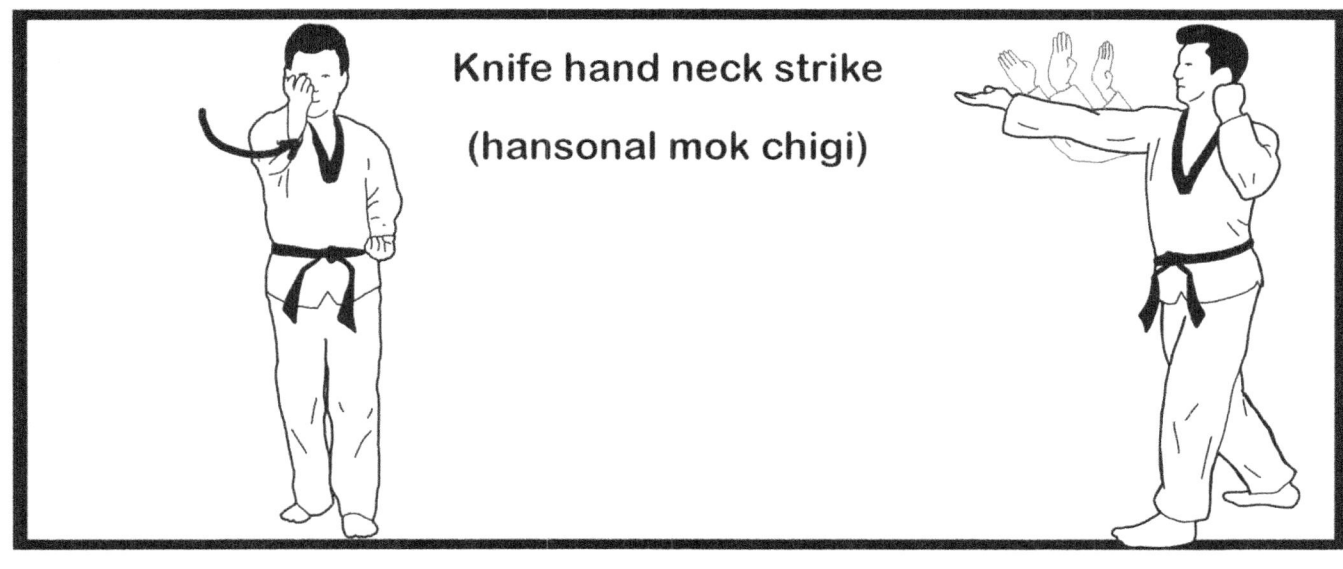

STRIKES & PUNCHES

Reverse middle punch (momtong baro jireugi)

High punch (ulgul bandai jireugi)

Hammer fist downward strike (ma jumeok naeryo chigi)

Elbow strike (palkup chigi)

Knife hand neck strike (hansonal mok chigi)

STRIKES & PUNCHES

Reverse back fist strike, supported (dong jumeok apchigi)

Spear hand strike (pyongsonkut jireugi)

Pulling uppercut to the chin (dangyo tok jireugi)

Double uppercut middle section punch (dujumeok jeochojireugi)

BASIC KICKS

- pushing kick (miro chagi)
- Side kick (yop chagi)
- Crescent kick (an chagi)
- Roundhouse kick (dolyo chagi)
- Front kick (apchuck ap chagi)
- Axe kick (naeryo chagi)

ADVANCED KICKS

- Spinning hook kick (pande dollyo chagi)
- Jumping roundhouse kick (twio dollyo chagi)
- Jumping front kick (twio ap chagi)
- Flying side kick (twio yop chagi)
- Double jumping front kick (twio kawi ap chagi)
- Jumping turning side kick (twio momdollyo yop chagi)

Animals in Taekwondo:

There are many different styles of martial arts around the world that have been developed over hundreds of years. Those martial arts were inspired by an array of movements from different sources, including animals. Some techniques were created by mimicking the movements of the animals and adapting them to the human body. These techniques include stances, blocks, hand attacks, and various kicks. Some techniques are based on the movements of the animals. For example, a back kick is inspired by a donkey kick. While other techniques are based on the shapes of the animals. For example, the bull horn block.

The following pages will show you a few of the techniques taken from the amazing animal world, that are used in Taekwondo.

The names of the techniques and their connection to animals may change between Taekwondo schools and styles, thus, you can find different versions. For example, you can find a "bear paw" described as a talon or a claw. The same applies to a back kick, it is sometimes referred to as a donkey kick, a mule kick or a horse kick. Another example is beom sugi - tiger stance which is sometimes named as a cat stance.

Animals in Taekwondo Stances

Horse riding stance (juchum sugi)

Crane stance (hakdari sugi)

Tiger stance (beom sugi)

Swallow shape knife-hand neck strike (jebipoom sonal mok chigi)

Animals in Taekwondo
hand techniques

Dropping bear paw (batangson nelyo makki)

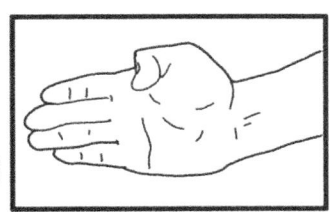

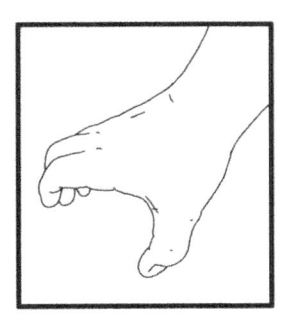

Eagle hand strike (agumson chigi)

Animals in Taekwondo
hand techniques and kicks

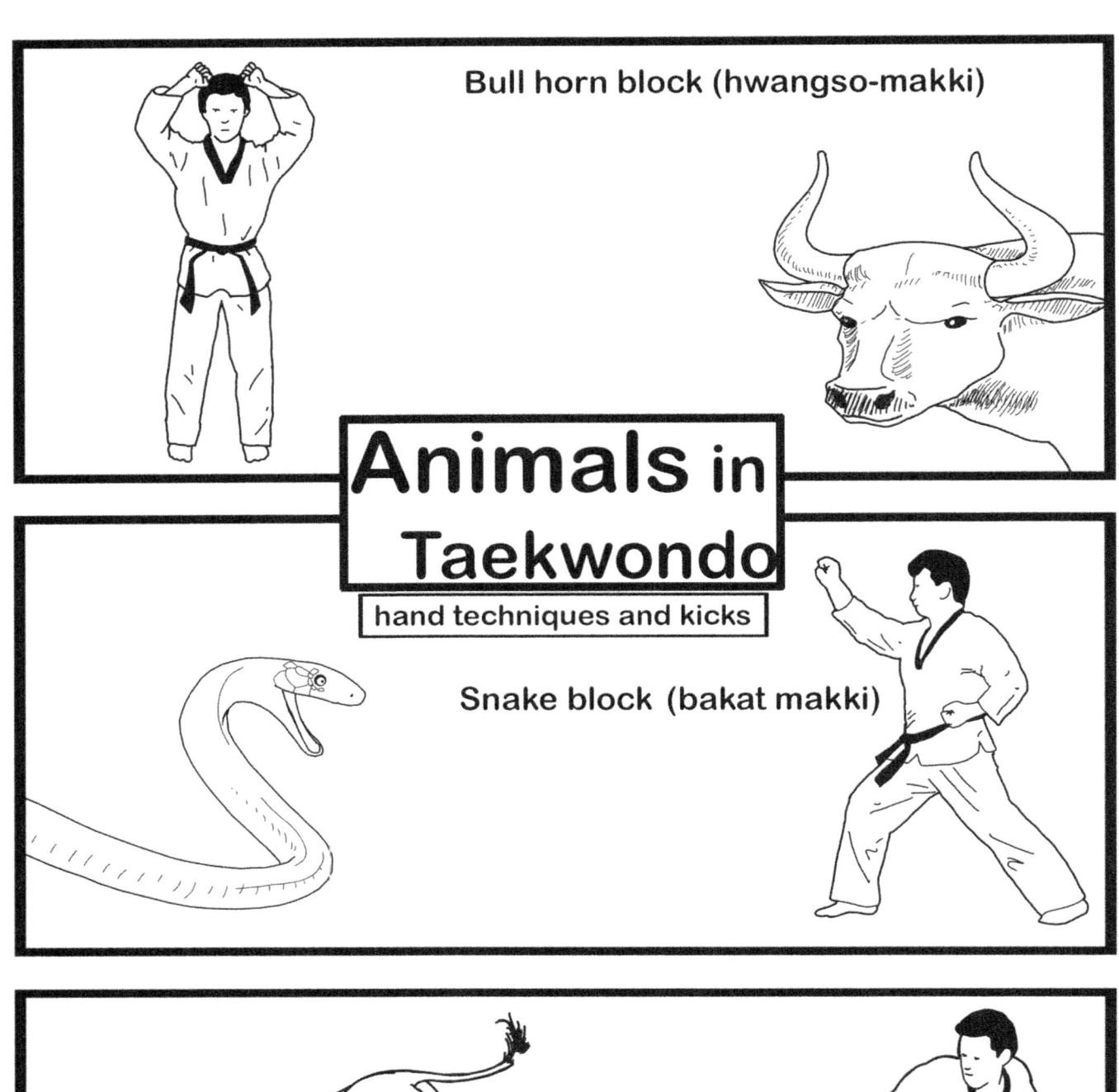

Bull horn block (hwangso-makki)

Snake block (bakat makki)

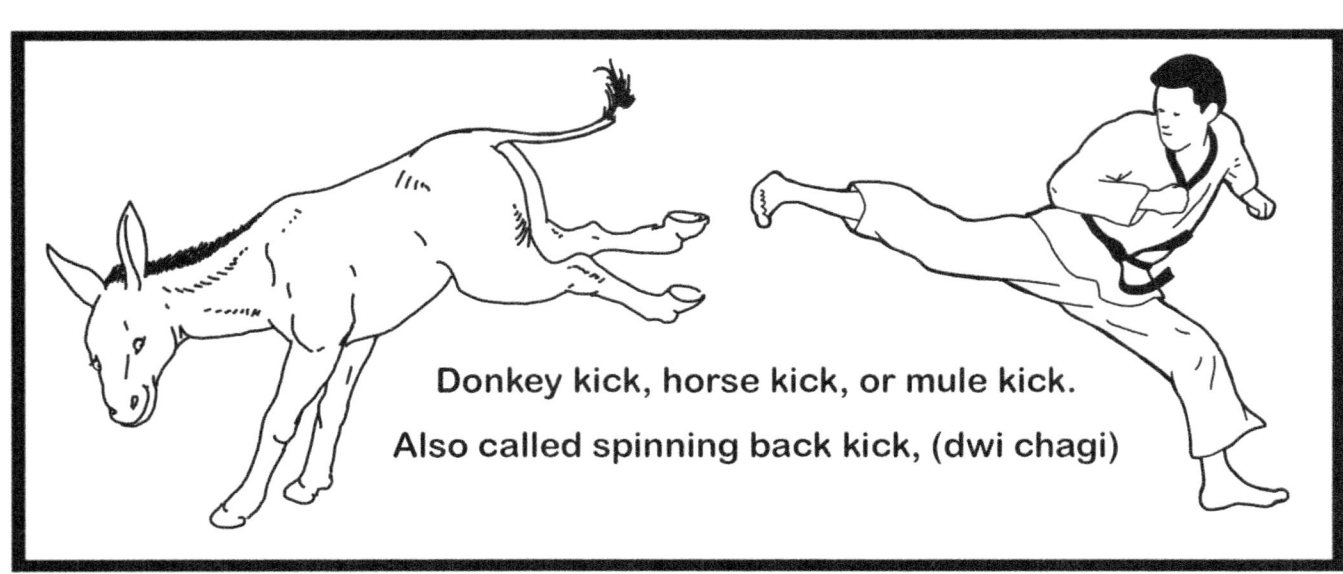

Donkey kick, horse kick, or mule kick.
Also called spinning back kick, (dwi chagi)

About the Authors:

MASTER JESSICA MANDEL is an International Master Instructor in TaeKwonDo and holder of a 6th degree DAN black belt certified by the Kukkiwon (Korea).
She has trained in TaeKwonDo for more than 38 years, has 30 years of teaching experience, and currently runs two full time gyms which attract an international body of students.
She is also a certified International Referee in poomsae (WT/ETU), has both competed and judged World and European competitions and is an International Referee in fighting.
In recognition to her contributions to the martial arts, the TaeKwonDo Hall of Fame recognized and honored Master Mandel as "Outstanding TaeKwonDo Instructor of Israel."

MASTER ALEX MAN is an International Master Instructor in TaeKwonDo and holder of a 5th degree DAN black belt certified by the Kukkiwon (Korea).
He has trained in martial arts for over 30 years and has taught Taekwondo for over 25 years.
For the last few years, he also practiced the Moo Duk Kwan Taekwondo.
Always a student, eager to learn the fascinating ways of the martial arts.
In addition, he is an illustrator and an author of children's books. This book is a great opportunity to combine those two passion for martial art and illustration.
He learned and taught Alternative Medicine (including Chinese medicine, Chinese acupuncture, and Korean acupuncture) for many years.
And most importantly, he's happily married and has 5 wonderful kids.

Dear reader,

Thank you so much for purchasing our book.

We hope you enjoyed it and learned from it.

We would greatly appreciate it if you could leave a review of our book on AMAZON.

Please feel free to check out our next book:

| Volume 2 – The Illustrated Guide to Palgwe Forms |

Hoping to see you soon,

Enjoy practicing Taekwondo!

Copyright 2018 Alex Man & Jessica Mandel

All rights reserved. No part of this publication may be reproduced, distributed, or transmitted in any form or by any means, including photocopying, recording, or other electronic or mechanical methods, without the prior written permission of the authors.

Printed in Great Britain
by Amazon